finish-free knits

No-Sew Garments in Classic Styles

KRISTEN TENDYKE

INTERWEAVE.
interweave.com

Editor	Ann Budd
Technical Editor	Therese Chynoweth
Photographer	Joe Hancock
Photo Stylist	Amy Pigliacampo
Hair and Makeup	Jessica Shinyeda
Art Director	Liz Quan
Interior Design	Karla Baker
Illustration	Gayle Ford
Production	Katherine Jackson

Interweave Press LLC
201 East Fourth Street
Loveland, CO 80537-5655 USA
Interweave.com

Printed in China by C & C Offset.

Library of Congress Cataloging-in-Publication Data

TenDyke, Kristen.
Finish-free knits : no-sew garments in classic styles /
Kristen TenDyke.
pages cm
Includes index.
ISBN 978-1-59668-488-1 (pbk.)
1. Knitting--Patterns. I. Title.
TT825.T423 2012
746.43'2--dc23
2012009824

10 9 8 7 6 5 4 3 2 1

ACKNOWLEDGMENTS

There is so much to be grateful for—so much time, effort, loving energy, and care has gone into bringing these pages into reality—it's impossible to list it all here.

I'm so thankful for having the opportunity to share these projects with you—thankful that you've picked up this book and found something worth knitting. Without you, this book could not be here. So, firstly, I thank you.

To those at Interweave: Ann Budd, Anne Merrow, Mary KinCannon, and those I didn't have the pleasure of working with personally—this book couldn't have been created without your guidance, talents, creativity, and time. Thank you.

To my knitters: Jessica Wright-Lichter, Kim Haesemeyer, Cecily MacDonald, and Kim Barnette—I'm so thankful for all the hard work and long hours you spent creating these sweaters. Without you, I would have probably lost my mind trying to find the time to get it all done.

The endless support, enthusiasm, and love I've received from my boyfriend, James; family; personal friends; and my knitter friends online, was beyond what I'd ever imagined. You all kept me moving and excited about the unfolding of the process and eager to see the book come into reality. I love you— thank you!

And lastly but, certainly, never least, I thank my dear mother, Diane—to whom I dedicate this book.

I bow.
Namasté   *Kristen*

contents

introduction

My grandmother had a great love for sewing. As a child, I admired the beautiful dolls and clothes she created. Throughout my elementary school years, she tried to teach me to sew many times, but I never did quite master the art of cutting out pieces of fabric and sewing them together, neither by hand nor machine. Everything I made turned out wonky—sewn with gaps in the fabric, with uneven seams, or it simply didn't fit. While the art of creating with fabric and thread wasn't for me, I did fall in love with the creation process—the process of transforming something simple into something unique and functional. The possibilities of what could be made by hand were endless.

Around the same time of my life, my mother taught me to crochet, which was a creative medium that I did enjoy. As a child who had no clue how to read a pattern, one of the things I loved about crocheting was being able to work around and around in circles, trying it on along the way, adding or subtracting stitches here and there, and ending up with something that fit with no sewing required.

When I learned to knit in my twenties, the first few sweaters I knitted from patterns were knitted in pieces—many of those pieces remain unsewn to this day. And the garments that I did seam were far from perfect. As I learned more about the construction of a sweater and began designing, I began to draw upon the things I loved about crochet—working around and around, adding or subtracting stitches here and there, and ending up with something that didn't need seaming.

While developing the designs for this book I focused on sweaters that I would enjoy knitting and wearing. They represent a variety of comfortable-casual designs, shaped and sized to fit a wide range of body shapes. Their names conjure a sense of well-being and contentment, which reflects how I hope you will feel while knitting and wearing these garments. Through these designs, I want to encourage more knitters to knit and complete sweaters.

I've known many knitters who limit themselves to hats, socks, and scarves because they're afraid or unwilling to sew pieces together.

Contained within these pages are sweater patterns for all levels of knitters. For the beginner, Ease (page 8) is a purl-free pattern that involves just knit stitches, a few simple decreases, and a few buttonholes. In other sweaters, there are easy-to-learn lace patterns that can be shaped without interrupting the stitch pattern; and sweaters worked side-to-side or from the top down that can be tried on along the way. The Serenity shrug (page 38) begins with a cable panel in the center back and ends with sleeves picked up along the edges of the panel and worked to the cuffs. For the more advanced knitter, a whole bunch of these patterns use interesting techniques for shaping sleeve caps and pockets. Above all, every design is worked seamlessly—no sewing is required. Each is completely constructed and shaped on the knitting needles; when the last stitch is bound off, you're done!

If you come across a technique that seems unfamiliar, I encourage you to give it a try. All the information you need to knit every garment in this book is included within these pages—either in the tips, stitch guides, or Glossary. Even if a particular pattern doesn't specifically point you to the Glossary, I encourage you go take a look. In it, you'll find general information about picking up stitches, weaving in ends, blocking, and attaching buttons. I also recommend browsing through the tips included within the garment instructions. In them, you're sure to learn pointers that will be useful for future projects.

ease 🍃 TANK

This super-easy top is worked entirely with knit stitches (no purls!), a few decreases, and a few buttonholes. The front and back plackets are worked back and forth in rows, then they are joined, and the body is worked in the round to the underarms. The front and back are then worked separately in rows to the shoulders. Buttonholes are added to the front shoulders; buttons are attached to the back shoulders and voilá—a simply beautiful sweater!

finished size
About 34 (37¼, 40¾, 44¼, 47¼, 50¾, 54¼)" (86.5 [94.5, 103.5, 112.5, 120, 129, 138] cm) bust circumference.
Tank shown measures 34" (86.5 cm).

yarn
Sportweight (#2 Fine).
SHOWN HERE: Classic Elite Allegoro (70% organic cotton, 30% linen; 152 yd [139 m]/50 g): #5656 larkspur, 5 (6, 6, 7, 8, 8, 8) balls.

needles
PLACKETS: size U.S. 4 (3.5 mm).
BODY: size U.S. 5 (3.75 mm): 24" circular (cir).
Adjust needle size if necessary to obtain the correct gauge.

notions
Stitch holder or waste yarn; marker (m); tapestry needle; four ½" (1.3 cm) buttons.

gauge
23 sts and 34 rnds = 4" (10 cm) in stockinette st on larger needles, worked in rounds.

22 sts and 38 rows = 4" (10 cm) in garter st on larger needles, worked in rows.

Front Placket

With smaller needles, use the long-tail method (see Glossary) to CO 99 (108, 118, 128, 137, 147, 157) sts. Slipping the first st of every row knitwise with yarn in back (kwise wyb), work in garter st (knit every row) for 18 rows, ending after a WS row. Place sts onto a holder or waste yarn. Cut yarn.

Back Placket

CO and work as for front placket but leave sts on needle and do not cut yarn.

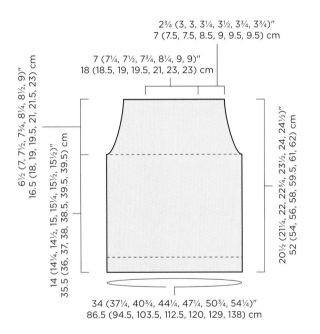

2¾ (3, 3, 3¼, 3½, 3¾, 3¾)"
7 (7.5, 7.5, 8.5, 9, 9.5, 9.5) cm

7 (7¼, 7½, 7¾, 8¼, 9, 9)"
18 (18.5, 19, 19.5, 21, 23, 23) cm

6½ (7, 7½, 7¾, 8¼, 8½, 9)"
16.5 (18, 19, 19.5, 21, 21.5, 23) cm

14 (14¼, 14½, 15, 15¼, 15½, 15½)"
35.5 (36, 37, 38, 38.5, 39.5, 39.5) cm

20½ (21¼, 22, 22¾, 23½, 24, 24½)"
52 (54, 56, 58, 59.5, 61, 62) cm

34 (37¼, 40¾, 44¼, 47¼, 50¾, 54¼)"
86.5 (94.5, 103.5, 112.5, 120, 129, 138) cm

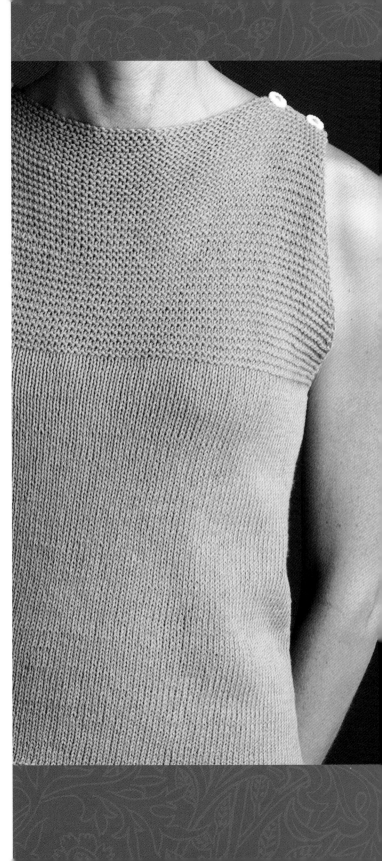

Body

JOINING RND: With larger cir needle and RS facing, knit to last st of back placket, sl 1 purlwise with yarn in back (pwise wyb), return held front placket sts onto empty end of needle in preparation to work a RS row (yarn tail is at needle tip), return slipped back placket st back to left-hand needle, k2tog (1 st from each placket), knit to last st of front placket, and join for working in rnds by working k2tog (1 st from each placket), being careful not to twist sts—196 (214, 234, 254, 272, 292, 312) sts. Pm for beg of rnd.

Cont in St st (knit all sts) until piece measures 14 (14¼, 14½, 15, 15¼, 15½, 15½)" [35.5 (36, 37, 38, 38.5, 39.5, 39.5) cm] from CO.

Divide for Front and Back

K96 (105, 115, 125, 133, 143, 153) sts for back, BO 3 (3, 4, 4, 5, 5, 6) sts, k95 (104, 113, 123, 131, 141, 150) sts for front, BO 3 (3, 4, 4, 5, 5, 6) sts, remove m. Place front sts onto holder or waste yarn to work later.

Back

Work 95 (104, 113, 123, 131, 141, 150) back sts in rows as foll:

Work 2 (0, 0, 0, 0, 0, 0) rows in garter st, slipping the first st of every row kwise wyb.

Shape Armholes

NEXT ROW: (RS) Sl 1 kwise wyb, knit to end.

DEC ROW: (WS) Sl 1 kwise wyb, k2tog, work to last 3 sts, ssk, k1—2 sts dec'd.

Rep the last 2 rows 0 (2, 6, 10, 12, 14, 17) more times—93 (98, 99, 101, 105, 111, 114) sts rem.

[Work 3 rows in garter st, then rep dec row] 12 (13, 12, 11, 11, 11, 12) times—69 (72, 75, 79, 83, 89, 90) sts rem.

Slipping the first st of every row kwise wyb, work even in garter st, until armholes measure 6½ (7, 7½, 7¾, 8¼, 8½, 9)" [16.5 (18, 19, 19.5, 21, 21.5, 23) cm] from dividing row, ending with a RS row.

With WS facing, BO all sts kwise.

Front

Return 95 (104, 113, 123, 131, 141, 150) held front sts onto larger needle and join yarn in preparation to work a RS row. Work as for back, ending before working the last RS row before the BO.

BUTTONHOLE ROW: (RS) Sl 1 kwise wyb, k1 (1, 2, 2, 2, 2, 2), work one-row buttonhole over 3 sts (see Glossary), k5 (6, 6, 7, 8, 9, 9), work one-row buttonhole over 3 sts, knit to last 15 (16, 17, 18, 19, 20, 20) sts, work one-row buttonhole over 3 sts, k5 (6, 6, 7, 8, 9, 9), work one-row buttonhole over 3 sts, knit to end—4 buttonholes worked.

With WS facing, BO all sts kwise.

Finishing

Sew buttons to back opposite buttonholes. Weave in loose ends. Block to measurements (see Glossary).

joy 🍃 LACE TUNIC

As the name implies, Joy is a pleasure to knit. Equally fun to wear, it can be paired with jeans, a skirt, or cool cotton shorts for trans-seasonal wear. Beginning with a picot cast-on, the body is worked in a lacy tube to the underarms, then box pleats are added at the bust. Extra stitches are cast on for the straps and the yoke is shaped in garter stitch. There is a lot of joy in simplicity!

finished size

About 29 (31½, 34¼, 37, 39½, 42¼, 45)" (73.5 [80, 87, 94, 100.5, 107.5, 114.5] cm) circumference at underarms and 39 (42, 45, 48, 51, 54, 57)" (99 [106.5, 114.5, 122, 129.5, 137, 145] cm) circumference at bust and lower edge.

Tank shown measures 31½" (80 cm) at underarms.

yarn

Worsted weight (#4 Medium).

SHOWN HERE: Knit Picks Simply Cotton Organic Worsted (100% organic cotton; 164 yd [150 m]/100 g): marshmallow, 3 (4, 4, 4, 5, 5, 5) skeins.

needles

BODY: size U.S. 7 (4.5 mm): 32" (80 cm) circular (cir) and set of 4 or 5 double-pointed (dpn).

STRAPS: size U.S. 4 (3.5 mm): 32" (80 cm) cir.

Adjust needle size if necessary to obtain the correct gauge.

notions

Markers (m); tapestry needle.

gauge

16 sts and 25 rnds = 4" (10 cm) in lace patt on larger needles.

18 sts and 36 rnds = 4" (10 cm) in garter st on smaller needles.

Body

With larger needle, *use the cable method (see Glossary) to CO 5 sts, BO 2 sts, sl st from right needle tip to left needle tip (1 picot made); rep from * until there are 52 (56, 60, 64, 68, 72, 76) picots—156 (168, 180, 192, 204, 216, 228) sts. Place marker (pm) and join for working in rnds, being careful not to twist sts.

NEXT RND: Purl all sts through their back loops (tbl).

Work Rnds 1–12 of Lace chart 6 times, then work Rnds 1–11 once again.

PLEAT RND: With smaller needles, k30 (30, 42, 42, 42, 42, 54), make right pleat (see box at right) over next 18 sts, k1, make left pleat over next 18 sts, knit to end—132 (144, 156, 168, 180, 192, 204) sts rem.

DEC RND: With smaller needle, p35 (35, 47, 47, 47, 47, 59), p3tog, purl to end—130 (142, 154, 166, 178, 190, 202) sts rem.

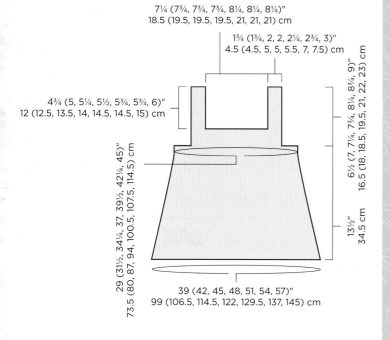

7¼ (7¾, 7¾, 7¾, 8¼, 8¼, 8¼)"
18.5 (19.5, 19.5, 19.5, 21, 21, 21) cm

1¾ (1¾, 2, 2, 2¼, 2¾, 3)"
4.5 (4.5, 5, 5, 5.5, 7, 7.5) cm

4¾ (5, 5¼, 5½, 5¾, 5¾, 6)"
12 (12.5, 13.5, 14, 14.5, 14.5, 15) cm

6½ (7, 7¼, 7¾, 8¼, 8¾, 9)"
16.5 (18, 18.5, 19.5, 21, 22, 23) cm

6½ (7, 7¼, 7¾, 8¼, 8¾, 9)"
16.5 (18, 18.5, 19.5, 21, 22, 23) cm

13½"
34.5 cm

29 (31½, 34¼, 37, 39½, 42¼, 45)"
73.5 (80, 87, 94, 100.5, 107.5, 114.5) cm

39 (42, 45, 48, 51, 54, 57)"
99 (106.5, 114.5, 122, 129.5, 137, 145) cm

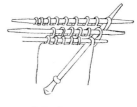

Lace

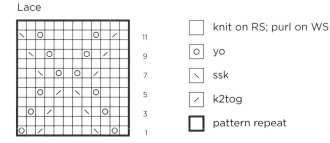

- ☐ knit on RS; purl on WS
- ○ yo
- \ ssk
- / k2tog
- ☐ pattern repeat

Divide for Armholes

BO 11 (10, 21, 20, 18, 16, 27) sts, k49 (51, 53, 55, 59, 63, 65) for front, BO 16 (20, 24, 28, 30, 32, 36) sts, k49 (51, 53, 55, 59, 63, 65) for back, BO 5 (10, 3, 8, 12, 16, 9) sts to end of rnd—49 (51, 53, 55, 59, 63, 65) sts rem each for front and back. Cut yarn.

CO for Straps

*Pm, turn work so WS is facing, use the cable method to CO 58 (62, 66, 70, 74, 78, 82) sts, pm, turn work so RS is facing, p49 (51, 53, 55, 59, 63, 65) front sts; rep from * once more for the second strap and back—214 (226, 238, 250, 266, 282, 294) sts total.

Shape Raglan

DEC RND: *K2tog, knit to 2 sts before next m, ssk; rep from * 3 more times—8 sts dec'd.

Purl 1 rnd. Rep the last 2 rnds 6 (6, 7, 8, 9, 11, 12) more times, then work dec rnd once more—150 (162, 166, 170, 178, 178, 182) sts rem; 42 (46, 48, 50, 52, 52, 54) sts for each strap; 33 (35, 35, 35, 37, 37, 37) sts each for front and back.

BO all sts purlwise.

Finishing

Weave in loose ends. Block to measurements (see Glossary).

harmony ❧ DRESS

A surprisingly simple lace pattern yields striking results in this little dress. Progressively smaller needles are used in the lace pattern between the hem and bust to create flattering flare in the body. To help prevent mistakes, place a marker after each 10-stitch pattern repeat and count stitches often to ensure errors are caught early on. For a chic accent, weave a colorful ribbon between the garter ridges at the top of the lace pattern.

finished size

About 29½ (32¾, 36¼, 39½, 43, 46¼, 49¾)" [75 (83, 92, 100.5, 109, 117.5, 126.5) cm] bust circumference.
Dress shown measures 32¾" (83 cm).

yarn

Worsted weight (#4 Medium).

SHOWN HERE: Classic Elite Yarn Classic Silk (50% cotton, 30% silk, 20% nylon; 135 yd [123 m]/50 g): #6967 wave break (teal), 5 (6, 6, 7, 7, 8, 9) balls.

needles

BODY: sizes U.S. 5, 6, 7, and 8 (3.75, 4, 4.5, and 5 mm): 32" (80 cm) circular (cir) each.

EDGING: size U.S. 5 (3.75 mm): 16" (40 cm) cir.

Adjust needle size if necessary to obtain the correct gauge.

notions

Markers (m); stitch holders or waste yarn; tapestry needle.

gauge

19 sts and 28 rnds = 4" (10 cm) in St st on size U.S. 6 (4 mm) needles, worked in rnds.

20 sts and 24 rnds = 4" (10 cm) in lace patt on size U.S. 5 (3.75 mm) needles, worked in rnds.

Skirt

With size U.S. 8 (5 mm) cir needle, use the long-tail method (see Glossary) to CO 130 (150, 170, 180, 200, 210, 230) sts. Being careful not to twist sts, join for working garter st (see Glossary) so that the joining bump is on the RS. Place marker (pm) to denote beg of rnd.

Knit 1 rnd, purl 1 rnd, then work Rnds 1–8 of Lace chart 5 times—40 rnds of lace total.

Change to size U.S. 7 (4.5 mm) cir needle and work Rnds 1–8 of chart 4 times.

Change to size U.S. 6 (4 mm) cir needle and work Rnds 1–8 of chart 3 (3, 3, 4, 4, 4, 4) times.

Change to size U.S. 5 (3.75 mm) cir needle and work Rnds 1–8 of chart 3 times.

Purl 1 rnd, knit 2 rnds, then purl 1 rnd—piece measures about 21 (21, 21, 22¼, 22¼, 22¼, 22¼)" (53.5 [53.5, 53.5, 56.5, 56.5, 56.5, 56.5] cm) from CO.

Lace

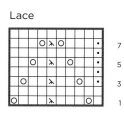

knit

· purl

o yo

⅄ sk2p

pattern repeat

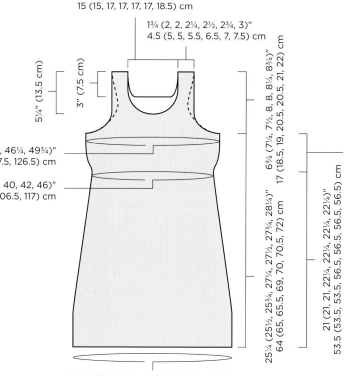

6 (6, 6¾, 6¾, 6¾, 6¾, 7¼)"
15 (15, 17, 17, 17, 17, 18.5) cm

1¾ (2, 2, 2¼, 2½, 2¾, 3)"
4.5 (5, 5, 5.5, 6.5, 7, 7.5) cm

5¼" (13.5 cm)

3" (7.5 cm)

29½ (32¾, 36¼, 39½, 43, 46¼, 49¾)"
75 (83, 92, 100.5, 109, 117.5, 126.5) cm

26 (30, 34, 36, 40, 42, 46)"
66 (76, 86.5, 91.5, 101.5, 106.5, 117) cm

6¾ (7¼, 7½, 8, 8, 8¼, 8¾)"
17 (18.5, 19, 20.5, 20.5, 21, 22) cm

4¼ (4½, 4¾, 5, 5¼, 5½, 6)"
11 (11.5, 12, 12.5, 13.5, 14, 15) cm

25¼ (25½, 25¾, 27¼, 27½, 27¾, 28¼)"
64 (65, 65.5, 69, 70, 70.5, 72) cm

21 (21, 21, 22¼, 22¼, 22¼, 22¼)"
53.5 (53.5, 53.5, 56.5, 56.5, 56.5, 56.5) cm

34¼ (39½, 44¾, 47¼, 52¾, 55¼, 60½)"
87 (100.5, 113.5, 120, 134, 140.5, 153.5) cm

checking gauge

When checking the gauge, I suggest using the same needle you'll be using for the actual garment. Not just the same-size needle, but the exact same needle because sometimes there are small differences, even between needles of the same size, that can cause unexpected differences in the finished gauge.

For the best results, swatch in rows if the gauge information specifies rows and swatch in rounds if the gauge information specifies rounds (or rnds). If both rows and rounds are specified (as for Bliss on page 24), test your gauge both ways as well.

Worked in Rows: Simply cast on at least 10% more stitches than the gauge calls for and work in the specified pattern stitch for 10% more rows than called for. This extra 10% allows you to avoid misshapen edge stitches when measuring your gauge. Be sure to measure the gauge in the center of the swatch where it's more likely to be an accurate representation of the garment.

Worked in Rounds: Use the circular or double-pointed needles called for in the pattern to cast on at least 10% more stitches than the gauge calls for, keeping a multiple of the number of stitches specified in the stitch pattern. Work across each row with the right side facing you, always slipping the stitches to the opposite needle tip at the end of every row and very loosely draping the yarn behind the work to bring it in position to work another right-side row. Every row will be knitted, and there will be loose strands of yarn across the wrong side of the work, as shown. After knitting a few rows, spread out the stitches along the cable part of the needle to ensure that the loose strands of yarn will accommodate the full width of the swatch.

For example, the gauge for the Harmony dress is 20 stitches and 24 rounds = 4" (10 cm) in lace pattern on size U.S. 5 (3.75 mm) needles. The lace pattern is worked over a multiple of 10 stitches, so you'd want to cast on 30 stitches for your gauge swatch.

For any lace pattern, you'll also want to check to see if there is a yarnover at the beginning or end of the pattern repeat. If so, cast on 1 additional stitch at that edge so that you'll have a stitch to anchor the yarnover and prevent it from inadvertently slipping off the needle. In this case, there is a yarnover at the end of the repeat on Row 1. Therefore, you'll want to work the swatch over 31 stitches. Work the swatch for at least 26 rounds, which is about 10% more rounds than specified in the gauge information.

After binding off the stitches, lay the swatch flat on a smooth surface and measure the stitch and row gauges before blocking it so you can compare it to the blocked gauge. Then wet the swatch in cool water and lay it flat to dry. I suggest wet-blocking (see Glossary) because if you ever plan on washing your garment, the wet-blocked gauge swatch will give you the most-accurate gauge for the desired fit. Once completely dry, measure the stitch and row gauges again. The after-blocking gauge should (hopefully) match the gauge in the pattern. Usually the stitch count is more important than the row count so, unless otherwise specified, match the stitch count as closely as possible. If you measure more stitches in your swatch than specified, try again with a larger needle size; if you measure fewer stitches, try again with a smaller needle size.

To double-check your gauge once you start knitting the garment, measure the gauge after knitting a few inches and you've gotten into the rhythm of knitting, if it matches the gauge you took before wet-blocking your swatch, then it will match the patterns gauge after blocking.

right side　　　*wrong side*

Bodice

Change to size U.S. 6 (4 mm) cir needle and knit 1 rnd.

Cont for your size as foll:

Sizes 29½ (32¾, 36¼, 43, 46¼)" only

INC RND: *K13 (25, 85, 50, 21), M1 (see Glossary); rep from *—140 (156, 172, 204, 220) sts.

Sizes 39½ (49¾)" only

INC RND: *[K23 (38), M1 (see Glossary)] 1 (2) time(s), k22 (39), M1; rep from *—188 (236) sts.

All sizes

Work 140 (156, 172, 188, 204, 220, 236) sts even in St st until piece measures 25¼ (25½, 25¾, 27¼, 27½, 27¾, 28¼)" (64 [65, 65.5, 69, 70, 70.5, 72] cm) from CO, ending the last rnd 6 (6, 6, 6, 7, 7, 7) sts before beg-of-rnd m.

Divide for Front and Back

BO 12 (12, 12, 12, 14, 14, 14) sts, work until there are 58 (66, 74, 82, 88, 96, 104) sts on the right-hand needle for front, BO 12 (12, 12, 12, 14, 14, 14) sts, work to end for back. Place front sts onto st holder or waste yarn to work later.

Back

Work 58 (66, 74, 82, 88, 96, 104) back sts as foll:

Purl 1 WS row.

Shape Armholes

BO 3 (3, 3, 3, 4, 4, 4) sts at beg of next 2 rows—52 (60, 68, 76, 80, 88, 96) sts rem.

DEC ROW 1: (RS) K1, k2tog, knit to last 3 sts, ssk, k1—2 sts dec'd.

DEC ROW 2: (WS) P1, ssp (see Glossary), purl to last 3 sts, p2tog, p1—2 sts dec'd.

Rep the last 2 rows 1 (1, 1, 2, 3, 4, 5) more time(s)—44 (52, 60, 64, 64, 68, 72) sts rem.

[Rep Dec Row 1, then purl 1 row] 4 (7, 8, 9, 8, 9, 9) times—36 (38, 44, 46, 48, 50, 54) sts rem.

Work even in St st until armholes measure 3¾ (4¼, 4½, 5, 5, 5¼, 5¾)" (9.5 (11, 11.5, 12.5, 12.5, 13.5, 14.5] cm) from dividing row, ending after a RS row.

Shape Neck

SET-UP ROW: (WS) P7 (8, 9, 10, 11, 12, 13), pm, p22 (22, 26, 26, 26, 26, 28) sts, pm, purl to end.

NEXT ROW: (RS) K1, M1, knit to first m, remove m, join a second ball of yarn, BO center 22 (22, 26, 26, 26, 26, 28) sts removing the second m, knit to last st, M1, k1—8 (9, 10, 11, 12, 13, 14) sts rem on each side.

Working each side separately, purl 1 WS row.

NEXT ROW: (RS) K1, M1, knit to 3 sts before neck edge, ssk, k1; on other side, k1, k2tog, work to last st, M1, k1—1 armhole st inc'd each side, 1 neck st dec'd each side.

Purl 1 WS row.

Rep the last 2 rows 2 more times—still 8 (9, 10, 11, 12, 13, 14) sts each side.

Cont even in St st until armholes measure 6¾ (7¼, 7½, 8, 8, 8¼, 8¾)" (17 [18.5, 19, 20.5, 20.5, 21, 22] cm), ending after a WS row.

Place all rem sts onto holders or waste yarn. Cut yarn and set aside.

Front

Return 58 (66, 74, 82, 88, 96, 104) held front sts onto size U.S. 6 (4 mm) cir needle and join yarn in preparation to work a WS row. Purl 1 WS row.

Shape Armholes

BO 3 (3, 3, 3, 4, 4, 4) sts at beg of next 2 rows—52 (60, 68, 76, 80, 88, 96) sts rem.

Note: Neck shaping is introduced while armhole shaping is in progress; read all the way through the foll sections before proceeding.

NEXT ROW: K1, k2tog, knit to last 3 sts, ssk, k1—2 sts dec'd.

Purl 1 WS row.

Rep the last 2 rows 3 (6, 7, 10, 11, 14, 16) more times and *at the same time* when armholes measure 1½ (2, 2¼, 2¾, 2¾, 3, 3½)" (3.8 [5, 5.5, 7, 7, 7.5, 9] cm), end after a RS row, shape neck as foll.

Shape Neck

Purl 1 WS row and *at the same time* pm each side of center 14 (14, 18, 18, 18, 18, 20) sts for neck.

NEXT ROW: (RS) Knit to first m, join a second ball of yarn and BO center 14 (14, 18, 18, 18, 18, 20) sts, knit to end.

Working each side separately, purl 1 WS row.

DEC ROW: (RS) Knit to 3 sts before neck edge, ssk, k1; on other side, k1, k2tog, knit to end—1 neck st dec'd each side.

Rep the last 2 rows 4 times.

[Work 3 rows even, then rep dec row] 2 times—8 (9, 10, 11, 12, 13, 14) sts rem each side after all shaping is complete.

Cont even until armholes measure 6¾ (7¼, 7½, 8, 8, 8¼, 8¾)" (17 [18.5, 19, 20.5, 20.5, 21, 22] cm), ending after a WS row.

Finishing

Join Shoulders

Return 8 (9, 10, 11, 12, 13, 14) held right back shoulder sts onto an empty needle. Hold corresponding 8 (9, 10, 11, 12, 13, 14) right front shoulder sts parallel to back sts so that RS face tog, and use the three-needle method (see Glossary) to BO sts tog. Rep for left shoulder.

Block to measurements (see Glossary).

Neck Trim

With shorter size U.S. 5 (3.75 mm) cir needle, RS facing, and beg at shoulder "seam," pick up and knit 140 (140, 148, 148, 148, 148, 152) sts evenly spaced (about 3 sts for every 4 rows along edges and 1 st in each BO st) around neck opening. Purl 1 rnd, knit 1 rnd. BO all sts purlwise.

Armhole Trim

With shorter size U.S. 5 (3.75 mm) cir needle, RS facing, and beg at base of armhole, pick up and knit 88 (93, 96, 100, 100, 103, 108) sts evenly spaced (about 3 sts for every 4 rows) around armhole opening. Purl 1 rnd, knit 1 rnd. BO all sts purlwise.

Weave in loose ends.

bliss ✤ TOP

This striking tunic features lace panels, wide ribs, and garter stitch worked in two different directions. The yoke is worked first from the cast-on at one sleeve, across the bodice, and ends with the bind-off at the other sleeve, with the underarms shaped with a few short-rows along the way. Stitches for the body are then picked up around the lower edge of the bodice and worked in a single piece to the hem. Lovely!

finished size

About 30½ (33¾, 37, 40, 43¼, 46½, 49¾)" (77.5 [85.5, 94, 101.5, 110, 118, 126.5] cm) bust circumference.

Tank shown measures 33¾" (85.5 cm).

yarn

Sportweight (#2 Fine).

SHOWN HERE: Elsebeth Lavold Hempathy (41% cotton, 34% hemp, 25% modal; 153 yd [140 m]/50 g), #024 lilac, 6 (7, 7, 8, 8, 9, 9) balls.

needles

BODICE: size U.S. 4 (3.5 mm): 32" (80 cm) circular (cir).

LOWER BODY AND SLEEVES: size U.S. 2 (2.75 mm): 24" (60 cm) cir and set of 4 double-pointed (dpn).

Adjust needle size if necessary to obtain the correct gauge.

notions

Markers (m); removable markers or safety pins; tapestry needle.

gauge

30 sts and 38 rnds = 4" (10 cm) in k3, p3 rib on smaller needle, worked in rnds.

24 sts and 32 rows = 4" (10 cm) in garter st (knit every row) on larger needle.

11 sts in lace panel = 2" (5 cm) wide on larger needle.

11 sts in lace panel = 1½" (3.8 cm) on smaller needle.

First Sleeve

With smaller dpn, use the long-tail method (see Glossary) to CO 90 (96, 108, 120, 126, 132, 144) sts. Place marker (pm) and join for working in rnds, being careful not to twist sts.

SET-UP RND: *K3, p3; rep from *.

Cont in rib as established until piece measures 3" (7.5 cm) from CO, ending 8 (9, 13, 17, 20, 21, 25) sts before beg-of-rnd m.

Bodice

Note: When working the short-rows (see Glossary) for the armhole shaping, do not hide the wraps.

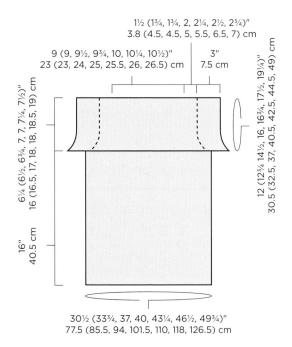

1½ (1¾, 1¾, 2, 2¼, 2½, 2¾)"
3.8 (4.5, 4.5, 5, 5.5, 6.5, 7) cm

9 (9, 9½, 9¾, 10, 10¼, 10½)"
23 (23, 24, 25, 25.5, 26, 26.5) cm

3"
7.5 cm

6¼ (6½, 6¾, 7, 7, 7¼, 7½)"
16 (16.5, 17, 18, 18, 18.5, 19) cm

12 (12¾, 14½, 16, 16¾, 17½, 19¼)"
30.5 (32.5, 37, 40.5, 42.5, 44.5, 49) cm

16"
40.5 cm

30½ (33¾, 37, 40, 43¼, 46½, 49¾)"
77.5 (85.5, 94, 101.5, 110, 118, 126.5) cm

reading a chart for rows and rounds

The Lace Panel chart for this garment is worked back and forth in rows (flat) for the bodice and in rounds for the skirt.

Working in Rows: When reading a chart for flat knitting, right-side (typically odd-numbered) rows are read from right to left; wrong-side (typically even-numbered) rows are read from left to right.

ROW 1: (RS) Working from right to left, p1, k2tog, [k1, yo] 2 times, k3, ssk, p1.

ROW 2: (WS) Working from left to right, k1, p9, k1.

Working in Rounds: When reading a chart for circular knitting, every row of the chart is considered a right-side row and is therefore read from right to left.

RND 1: (RS) (same as working in rows) Working from right to left, p1, k2tog, [k1, yo] 2 times, k3, ssk, p1.

RND 2: (RS) Working from right to left, p1, k9, p1.

Lace Panel

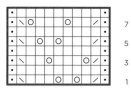

☐ knit on RS; purl on WS

· purl on RS; knit on WS

○ yo

╱ k2tog

╲ ssk

☐ pattern repeat

Shape First Armhole

SET-UP ROW: With larger cir needle, BO 19 (21, 29, 37, 43, 45, 53) sts, removing m when you come to it—1 st rem on right needle tip; wrap the next st, turn work, so WS is facing, k1, turn work—71 (75, 79, 83, 83, 87, 91) sts rem.

SHORT-ROW 1: With RS facing, knit to wrapped st, knit the wrapped st, wrap next st, turn work so WS is facing, knit to end.

Rep this short-row 1 (2, 3, 3, 3, 4, 4) more time(s).

Establish lace patt for your size as foll.

Sizes 30½ (33¾, 37)" only

NEXT ROW: (RS) K4 (5, 6), pm, work 11 sts according to Row 1 of Lace Panel chart, pm, k5, pm, work 11 sts according to Row 1 of chart, pm, k9 (11, 13), pm, work 11 sts according to Row 1 of chart, pm, k5, pm, work 11 sts according to Row 1 of chart, k4 (5, 6).

Sizes 40 (43¼, 46½)" only

DEC ROW: (RS) K6 (6, 7), pm, work 11 sts according to Row 1 of Lace Panel chart, pm, k3, k2tog, k2, pm, work 11 sts according to Row 1 of chart, pm, k13 (13, 15), pm, work 11 sts according to Row 1 of chart, pm, k2, k2tog, k3, pm, work 11 sts according to Row 1 of chart, pm, k6 (6, 7)—81 (81, 85) sts rem.

Size 49¾" only

DEC ROW: (RS) K7, pm, work 11 sts according to Row 1 of Lace Panel chart, pm, k3, k2tog, k3, pm, work 11 sts according to Row 1 of chart, pm, k3, k2tog, k7, k2tog, k3, pm, work 11 sts according to Row 1 of chart, pm, k3, k2tog, k3,

pm, work 11 sts according to Row 1 of chart, pm, k7—87 sts rem.

All sizes

Cont even in patt as established, maintaining sts between and outside lace panels in garter st (knit every row).

SHORT-ROW 2: With WS facing, k1, wrap next st, turn work so RS is facing, k1.

SHORT-ROW 3: With WS facing, knit to wrapped st, knit wrapped st, wrap next st, turn work so RS is facing, knit to end.

Rep the last short-row 1 (2, 3, 3, 3, 4, 4) more time(s).

Cont as established until piece measures 4½ (4¾, 4¾, 5, 5¼, 5½, 5¾)" (11.5 [12, 12, 12.5, 13.5, 14, 14.5] cm) from CO, ending after a WS row and measuring along the center of the work where no short-rows have been worked.

Divide for Neck

With RS facing and keeping in patt, work 35 (37, 39, 40, 40, 42, 43) sts, join a second ball of yarn and BO 1 st, then work to end—35 (37, 39, 40, 40, 42, 43) sts rem each side.

Working each side separately, cont even until piece measures 9 (9, 9½, 9¾, 10, 10¼, 10½)" (23 [23, 24, 25, 25.5, 26, 26.5] cm) from neck divide, ending after a WS row.

JOINING ROW: (RS) Work to neck edge, use the backward-loop method (see Glossary) to CO 1 st, then work to end with the same ball of yarn—71 (75, 79, 81, 81, 85, 87) sts.

Cut off other ball of yarn and cont as established until piece measures 1½ (1¾, 1¾, 2, 2¼, 2½, 2¾)" (3.8 [4.5, 4.5, 5, 5.5, 6.5, 7] cm) from joining row, ending after a WS row.

Shape Second Armhole

SHORT-ROW 1: With RS facing, k3 (4, 5, 5, 5, 6, 6), wrap next st, turn work so WS is facing, knit to end.

SHORT-ROW 2: With RS facing, knit to 1 st before wrapped st, wrap next st, turn work so WS is facing, knit to end.

Rep the last short-row 1 (2, 3, 3, 3, 4, 4) more time(s).

Cont for your size as foll:

Sizes 30½ (33¾, 37)" only

NEXT ROW: (RS) Work to end as established, removing markers.

Sizes 40 (43¼, 46½)" only

INC ROW: (RS) K6 (6, 7), remove m, work 11 sts according to next row of Lace Panel chart, remove m, k3, M1 (see Glossary), k3, remove m, work 11 sts according to next row of chart, remove m, k13 (13, 15), remove m, work 11 sts according to next row of chart, remove m, k3, M1, k3, remove m, work 11 sts according to next row of chart, pm remove m k6 (6, 7)—83 (83, 87) sts.

Size 49¾" only

INC ROW: (RS) K7, remove m, work 11 sts according to next row of Lace Panel chart, remove m, k3, M1 (see Glossary), k4, remove m, work 11 sts according to next row of chart, remove m, k4, M1, k7, M1, k4, remove m, work 11 sts according to next row of chart, k4, M1, k3, remove m, work 11 sts according to next row of chart, k7—91 sts.

Second Sleeve

With dpn, use the cable method (see Glossary) to CO 19 (21, 29, 37, 43, 45, 53) sts—90 (96, 108, 120, 126, 132, 144) sts. Join for working in rnds (do not pm yet).

NEXT RND: P2 (1, 1, 0, 2, 3, 1), k3 (3, 3, 2, 3, 3, 3), p3, [k3, p3] 0 (0, 1, 1, 2, 2, 3) time(s), pm for beg of rnd.

NEXT RND: *K3, p3; rep from *.

Cont in rib as established for 3" (7.5 cm). BO all sts in patt.

Body

Place a removable marker at center bodice front and center bodice back.

With smaller cir needle and beg just before the armhole BO, *pick up and knit 19 (21, 29, 37, 43, 45, 53) sts along the underarm BO sts, then 47 (52, 54, 56, 59, 64, 66) sts evenly spaced along the side edge of the bodice to the center m, remove m, pick up and knit 48 (53, 55, 57, 60, 65, 67) sts evenly spaced to next set of underarm sts; rep from * once, then k0 (0, 0, 2, 0, 0, 0), p2 (3, 1, 3, 2, 3, 1), [k3, p3] 1 (1, 2, 3, 3, 3, 4) time(s), pm for beg of rnd—228 (252, 276, 300, 324, 348, 372) sts total.

SET-UP RND: [K3, p3] 8 (9, 10, 11, 12, 13, 14) times, k3, p2, work 11 sts according to Row 1 of Lace Panel chart, p2, [k3, p3] 16 (18, 20, 22, 24, 26, 28) times, k3, p2, work 11 sts according to Row 1 of chart, p2, [k3, p3] 8 (9, 10, 11, 12, 13, 14) times.

Cont in patt as established until piece measures 15" (38 cm) from pick-up rnd, ending after an even-numbered rnd of chart.

NEXT RND: *K3, p3; rep from *.

Cont in k3, p3 rib as established for 1" (2.5 cm). Loosely BO all sts in patt.

Finishing

Weave in loose ends. Block to measurements (see Glossary).

peace TUNIC

This lace-panel tunic can be worn casual to dressy, depending on how it's styled. Beginning at the lower edge, it's knitted in rounds to the base of the deep front neck. Then it's worked back and forth in rows to the armholes, at which point the fronts and back are divided and worked separately to the shoulders. A few stitches are joined at the armhole edges for the shoulders, then the leaf panels continue to the back neck.

finished size

About 32 (35½, 39½, 43, 46½, 50, 54)" (81.5 [90.5, 100, 109, 118, 127, 136] cm) bust circumference.
Tunic shown measures 35½" (90.5 cm).

yarn

Worsted weight (#4 Medium).

SHOWN HERE: Classic Elite Yarns Premiere (50% pima cotton, 50% Tencel; 108 yd [99 m]/50 g): #5222 dusty miller (pale green), 6 (7, 8, 8, 9, 10, 11) skeins.

needles

Size U.S. 4 (3.5 mm): 32" (80 cm) circular (cir), straight, and double-pointed (dpn).

Adjust needle size if necessary to obtain the correct gauge.

notions

Markers (m); stitch holders or waste yarn; tapestry needle.

gauge

22 sts and 27 rnds = 4" (10 cm) in Rev St st, worked in rnds.

16 sts in lace panel = 2" (5 cm) wide.

Body

With cir needle, use the long-tail method (see Glossary) to CO 196 (216, 236, 256, 276, 296, 316) sts. Being careful not to twist sts, join for working Rev St st (see Glossary) so that the joining bump is on the RS. Place marker (pm) to denote beg of rnd.

[Knit 1 rnd, then purl 1 rnd] 2 times.

SET-UP RND: P24 (29, 34, 39, 44, 49, 54), pm, work 16 sts according to Row 1 of Left Lace Panel chart, pm, p20, pm, work 16 sts according to Row 1 of Right Lace Panel chart, pm, p50 (59, 68, 77, 86, 95, 104), pm for first back dart, p44 (46, 48, 50, 52, 54, 56), pm for second back dart, p26 (30, 34, 38, 42, 46, 50).

Cont in patt as established until piece measures 2" (5 cm) from CO, ending after an odd-numbered rnd of charts.

Shape Waist

DEC RND: Purl to first m, sl m, work 16 sts as charted, slip marker (sl m), p2tog, purl to 2 sts before next m, ssp (see Glossary), sl m, work 16 sts as charted, sl m, purl to dart m, sl m, p2tog, purl to 2 sts before next dart m, ssp, sl m, purl to end—4 sts dec'd.

Work 9 (9, 9, 11, 11, 11, 11) rnds even.

Rep the last 10 (10, 10, 12, 12, 12, 12) rnds 5 (6, 7, 0, 1, 2, 3) more time(s)—172 (188, 204, 252, 268, 284, 300) sts rem.

Cont for your size as foll.

Sizes 32 (35½, 43, 46½, 50, 54)" only
Rep dec rnd, then work 7 (7, 9, 9, 9, 9) rnds even.

Rep the last 8 (8, 10, 10, 10, 10) rnds 1 (0, 6, 5, 4, 3) more time(s)—164 (184, 224, 244, 264, 284) sts rem.

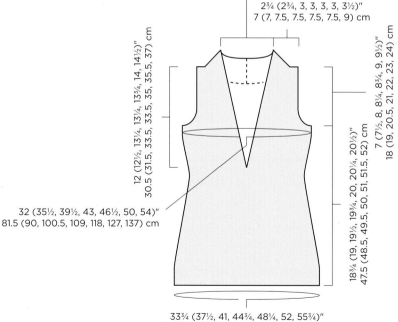

6½ (7, 7, 7½, 8½, 9, 9)"
16.5 (18, 18, 19, 21.5, 23, 23) cm

2¾ (2¾, 3, 3, 3, 3, 3½)"
7 (7, 7.5, 7.5, 7.5, 7.5, 9) cm

12 (12½, 13¼, 13¼, 13¾, 14, 14½)"
30.5 (31.5, 33.5, 33.5, 35, 35.5, 37) cm

7 (7½, 8, 8¼, 8¾, 9, 9½)"
18 (19, 20.5, 21, 22, 23, 24) cm

32 (35½, 39½, 43, 46½, 50, 54)"
81.5 (90, 100.5, 109, 118, 127, 137) cm

18¾ (19, 19½, 19¾, 20, 20¼, 20½)"
47.5 (48.5, 49.5, 50, 51, 51.5, 52) cm

33¾ (37½, 41, 44¾, 48¼, 52, 55¾)"
85.5 (95.5, 104, 113.5, 122.5, 132, 141.5) cm

Left Lace

(chart with row numbers 1, 3, 5, 7, 9, 11)

Right Lace

(chart with row numbers 1, 3, 5, 7, 9, 11)

☐	knit on RS; purl on WS
○	yo
⋏	k3tog
⅄	sl 3 sts individually kwise, insert left needle tip in the fronts of these slipped sts, then knit them tog through their back loops
☐	pattern repeat

All sizes

Rep dec rnd—160 (180, 200, 220, 240, 260, 280) sts rem.

NEXT RND: Keeping in patt, work 82 (92, 102, 112, 122, 132, 142) sts for front, pm for side, work 78 (88, 98, 108, 118, 128, 138) sts for back.

Cut yarn.

Divide for Neck

Slip 41 (46, 51, 56, 61, 66, 71) left front sts so needle tips are between the 2 center purl sts. Rejoin yarn to right front in preparation to work a RS row—41 (46, 51, 56, 61, 66, 71) sts each front; 78 (88, 98, 108, 118, 128, 138) sts for back. Rows beg at center front.

Cont working back and forth in rows as foll.

Shape Back Waist and Front Neck

DEC/INC ROW: (RS) P1, remove m, work 16 sts as charted, sl m, p2tog, work in Rev St st (purl RS row, knit WS rows) to next back dart m, sl m, M1P (see Glossary), work in Rev St st to next dart m, M1P, sl m, work in Rev St st to 2 sts before next m, ssp, sl m, work 16 sts as charted, remove m, p1—1 st dec'd on each front; 2 sts inc'd on back.

Work 5 rows even as established.

Rep the last 6 rows 4 more times, removing back dart markers on the last row—36 (41, 46, 51, 56, 61, 66) sts for each front; 88 (98, 108, 118, 128, 138, 148) sts for back.

NECK DEC ROW: (RS) P1, work 16 sts as charted, sl m, p2tog, work in Rev St st to 2 sts before next chart m, ssp, sl m, work 16 sts as charted, p1—35 (40, 45, 50, 55, 60, 65) sts rem for each front.

Work 3 rows even as established, ending after a WS row.

Divide for Armholes

(RS) P1, work 16 sts as charted, sl m, *work in Rev St st to 5 (6, 6, 7, 7, 8, 8) sts before side m, BO 10 (12, 12, 14, 14, 16, 16) sts removing m; rep from * once, work in Rev St st to next chart m, sl m, work 16 sts as charted, p1—30 (34, 39, 43, 48, 52, 57) sts rem for each front; 78 (86, 96, 104, 114, 122, 132) sts rem for back.

Leaving yarn attached to left front sts, place left and right front sts onto holders or waste yarn. Make note of the last row worked of lace panels.

Back

Join a new ball of yarn in preparation to work a WS row across 78 (86, 96, 104, 114, 122, 132) back sts.

Shape Armholes

Work 1 WS row.

DEC ROW: (RS) P1, p2tog, purl to last 3 sts, ssp, p1—2 sts dec'd.

Rep the last 2 rows 1 (4, 8, 10, 14, 16, 20) more time(s)—74 (76, 78, 82, 84, 88, 90) sts rem.

[Work 3 rows even, then rep dec row] 4 (4, 3, 3, 2, 2, 1) time(s)—66 (68, 72, 76, 80, 84, 88) sts rem.

Cont even in Rev St st until armholes measure 4 (4½, 5, 5¼, 5¾, 6, 6½)" (10 [11.5, 12.5, 13.5, 14.5, 15, 16.5] cm), ending after a WS row.

Shape Neck

With RS facing, p23 (23, 25, 25, 27, 27, 29), join a second ball of yarn and BO center 20 (22, 22, 26, 26, 30, 30) sts, purl to end—23 (23, 25, 25, 27, 27, 29) sts rem each side.

Work each side separately as foll:

NEXT ROW: (WS) Knit to BO sts; on other side BO 8 (8, 8, 8, 10, 10, 10) sts, knit to end.

NEXT ROW: Purl to BO sts; on other side, BO 8 (8, 8, 8, 10, 10, 10) sts, purl to end—15 (15, 17, 17, 17, 17, 19) sts rem each side.

NEXT ROW: Knit to BO sts; on other side, BO 6 sts, knit to end.

NEXT ROW: Purl to BO sts; on other side, BO 6 sts, purl to end—9 (9, 11, 11, 11, 11, 13) sts rem each side.

Knit 1 WS row.

DEC ROW: (RS) Purl to 2 sts before neck edge, ssp; on other side, p2tog, purl to end—1 st dec'd each side.

Rep the last 2 rows 6 more times—2 (2, 4, 4, 4, 4, 6) sts rem each side.

Place rem sts onto holders or waste yarn. Cut yarn, leaving a 12" (30.5 cm) tail for the right shoulder.

Left Front

Return 30 (34, 39, 43, 48, 52, 57) held left front sts to straight needle in preparation to work a WS row. Work 1 WS row as established.

Note: Neck shaping begins while armhole shaping is in progress; read all the way through the foll sections before proceeding.

Shape Armhole

DEC ROW: (RS) P1, p2tog, work to end—1 st dec'd at armhole.

Work 1 WS row as established.

Rep the last 2 rows 1 (4, 8, 10, 14, 16, 20) more time(s).

[Work 3 rows even, then rep dec row] 4 (4, 3, 3, 2, 2, 1) time(s) and *at the same time* on first armhole dec row, shape neck as foll.

Shape Neck

DEC ROW: (RS) Working armhole dec as specified, work to 2 sts before chart m, ssp, sl m, work 16 sts as charted, p1—1 st dec'd at neck.

[Work 5 rows even, rep neck dec row, work 3 rows even, rep neck dec row] 1 (2, 2, 3, 4, 5, 5) time(s)—21 (20, 22, 22, 22, 22, 24) sts rem after all shaping is complete.

Cont for your size as foll.

Size 32" only
Work 3 rows even, ending after a WS row.

Rep neck dec row—20 sts rem.

All sizes
Work even until armhole measures 7 (7½, 8, 8¼, 8¾, 9, 9½)" (18 [19, 20.5, 21, 22, 23, 24] cm), ending after a WS row. Cut yarn, leaving a 12" (30. 5 cm) tail.

Left Neck Extension

Pm at center of back neck.

With RS facing, place the first 2 (2, 4, 4, 4, 4, 6) front sts onto one dpn, place the corresponding 2 (2, 4, 4, 4, 4, 6) left back sts onto a second dpn, then use the tail and the three-needle method (see Glossary) to BO the sts tog—18 front sts rem.

ROW 1: (RS) With empty needle, pick up and knit 1 st from back neck edge and place it onto the left needle tip, p2tog, work 16 sts as charted, p1.

ROW 2: Keeping in patt, work to last st, sl 1 purlwise with yarn in front (pwise wyf).

Rep these 2 rows to m at the center back neck, ending after a RS row.

Place all sts onto holder. Cut yarn.

Right Front

Return 30 (34, 39, 43, 48, 52, 57) held right front sts onto straight needle and join yarn in preparation to work a WS row. Work 1 WS row as established.

Note: Neck shaping begins while armhole shaping is in progress; read all the way through the foll sections before proceeding.

Shape Armhole

DEC ROW: (RS) Work to last 3 sts, ssp, p1—1 st dec'd at armhole.

Work 1 WS row as established.

Rep the last 2 rows 1 (4, 8, 10, 14, 16, 20) more time(s).

[Work 3 rows even, then rep dec row] 4 (4, 3, 3, 2, 2, 1) time(s) and *at the same time* on the first armhole dec row, cont to shape neck as foll.

Shape Neck

DEC ROW: (RS) P1, work 16 sts as charted, sl m, p2tog, purl to end, working armhole dec as specified—1 st dec'd at neck.

[Work 5 rows even, rep neck dec row, work 3 rows even, rep neck dec row] 1 (2, 2, 3, 4, 5, 5) time(s)—21 (20, 22, 22, 22, 22, 24) sts rem after all shaping is complete.

Cont for your size as foll.

Size 32" only

Work 3 rows even, ending after a WS row.

Rep neck dec row—20 sts rem.

All sizes

Work even until armhole measures 7 (7½, 8, 8¼, 8¾, 9, 9½)" (18 [19, 20.5, 21, 22, 23, 24] cm), ending after a WS row. Do not cut yarn.

Right Neck Extension

ROW 1: (RS) Work to last 2 (2, 4, 4, 4, 4, 6) sts, place the last 2 (2, 4, 4, 4, 4, 6) sts onto one dpn, place the corresponding 2 (2, 4, 4, 4, 4, 6) back sts onto a second dpn, then use the yarn tail and the three-needle method to BO the sts tog, then, with working needle, pick up and knit 1 st—19 sts rem: 18 front sts and 1 back st.

ROW 2: (WS) Ssk, work to end—1 st dec'd.

ROW 3: P1, work 16 sts as charted, sl 1 pwise wyb, pick up and knit 1 st from back neck edge.

Rep the last 2 rows to m at center back neck, ending after a RS row and omitting the picked up st at the end of the last RS row.

Return 18 held left front sts onto working needle so that tip of needle is facing the same direction as the right front needle when held parallel. With RS tog, use the three-needle method to BO sts tog so seam is on the WS.

Finishing

Neck Trim

With cir needle, RS facing, and beg at center back neck seam, pick up and knit 3 sts for every 4 rows evenly spaced along neck edge to center front, pick up 1 st at center of V, pm, pick up 1 more st at center of V, then pick up 3 sts for every 4 rows evenly spaced along neck edge to center back—about 164 (171, 176, 181, 190, 195, 201) sts total. Pm and join for working in rnds.

RND 1: Purl to 2 sts before center front m, ssp, sl m, p2tog, purl to end—2 sts dec'd.

RND 2: Knit.

BO while working as for Rnd 1.

Armhole Trim

With dpn, RS facing, and beg at center of underarm BO sts, pick up and knit 78 (84, 88, 94, 98, 104, 108) sts (about 1 st in each BO st and 3 sts for each 4 rows) evenly spaced around armhole opening. Pm and join for working in rnds. Purl 1 rnd, then knit 1 rnd.

BO all sts purlwise.

Weave in loose ends. Block to measurements (see Glossary).

serenity 🍃 SHRUG

This is the perfect garment to add a touch of evening-night-out elegance. It begins with a cable panel at the center back, which is worked with two strands of yarn held together, then stitches are picked up along the sides of the panel, and the sleeves are worked (with a single strand of yarn) to the cuffs. A stretchy picot bind-off around the cuffs and body opening provides a feminine edge with a comfy fit.

finished size

About 33½ (37½, 40½, 44½, 49, 52, 55)" (85 [95, 103, 113, 124.5, 132, 139.5] cm) circumference around opening.

Shrug shown measures 37½" (95 cm).

yarn

Worsted weight (#4 Medium).

SHOWN HERE: Bijou Basin Ranch Bliss (50% yak, 50% cormo; 150 yd [137 m]/2 oz [56 g]): #13 steel, 4 (4, 5, 5, 6, 6, 7) skeins.

needles

CENTER PANEL: size U.S. 9 (5.5 mm).

BODY, SLEEVES, AND EDGING: size U.S. 7 (4.5 mm): 32" (80 cm) circular (cir) and set of 4 double-pointed (dpn).

Adjust needle size if necessary to obtain the correct gauge.

notions

Markers (m); cable needle (cn); tapestry needle.

gauge

20 sts and 32 rows = 4" (10 cm) in garter st on smaller needles.

24 sts and 24 rows in cable panel = 6" (15 cm) wide and 4¼" (11 cm) long on larger needles with two strands of yarn held tog.

NOTES

→ *To obtain the correct fit of this garment, hold (or ask a friend to hold) the end of a length of cotton string at the back of your neck, bring the other end of the string over your shoulder to your front, under one of your arms, across your mid back, below your other arm to your front, over your second shoulder and back to the center of your back neck. Measure that length of string and add 1" to 2" (2.5 to 5 cm) of ease.*

→ *Two strands of yarn are held together for the center panel; a single strand is used elsewhere.*

Center Panel

With larger needle and two strands of yarn held tog, use the long-tail method (see Glossary) to CO 28 (28, 30, 30, 32, 32, 34) sts.

SET-UP ROW: (WS) Work 2 (2, 3, 3, 4, 4, 5) sts in Rev St st (knit WS rows; purl RS rows), place marker (pm), work 24 sts according to Row 1 (1, 19, 19, 1, 1, 19) of Cable chart, pm, work in Rev St st to end.

Cont as established until a total of 51 (51, 63, 63, 75, 75, 87) rows have been worked, ending after Row 3 (3, 9, 9, 3, 3, 9) of chart. BO all sts, cut one strand of yarn and pull that tail through the last loop. Place rem single-strand loop onto smaller cir needle.

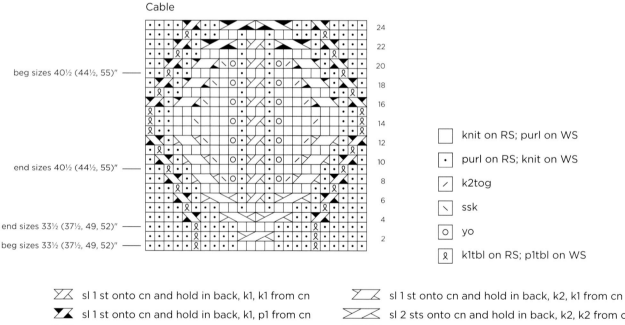

Cable

☐	knit on RS; purl on WS
•	purl on RS; knit on WS
╱	k2tog
╲	ssk
○	yo
℞	k1tbl on RS; p1tbl on WS

sl 1 st onto cn and hold in back, k1, k1 from cn
sl 1 st onto cn and hold in back, k1, p1 from cn
sl 1 st onto cn and hold in front, p1, k1 from cn
sl 2 sts onto cn and hold in front, p1, k2 from cn
sl 1 st onto cn and hold in back, k2, p1 from cn
sl 2 sts onto cn and hold in front, k1, k2 from cn

sl 1 st onto cn and hold in back, k2, k1 from cn
sl 2 sts onto cn and hold in back, k2, k2 from cn
sl 2 sts onto cn and hold in front, k2, k2 from cn
sl 2 sts onto cn and hold in back, k2, p2 from cn
sl 2 sts onto cn and hold in front, p2, k2 from cn

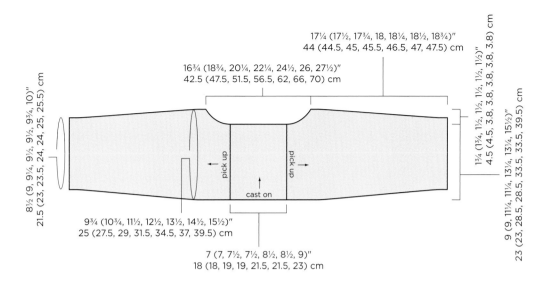

16¾ (18¾, 20¼, 22¼, 24½, 26, 27½)"
42.5 (47.5, 51.5, 56.5, 62, 66, 70) cm

17¼ (17½, 17¾, 18, 18¼, 18½, 18¾)"
44 (44.5, 45, 45.5, 46.5, 47, 47.5) cm

8½ (9, 9¼, 9½, 9½, 9¾, 10)"
21.5 (23, 23.5, 24, 24, 25, 25.5) cm

1¾ (1¾, 1½, 1½, 1½, 1½, 1½)"
4.5 (4.5, 3.8, 3.8, 3.8, 3.8, 3.8) cm

9 (9, 11¼, 11¼, 13¼, 13¼, 15½)"
23 (23, 28.5, 28.5, 33.5, 33.5, 39.5) cm

pick up

pick up

cast on

9¾ (10¾, 11½, 12½, 13½, 14½, 15½)"
25 (27.5, 29, 31.5, 34.5, 37, 39.5) cm

7 (7, 7½, 7½, 8½, 8½, 9)"
18 (18, 19, 19, 21.5, 21.5, 23) cm

Left Body

Cont with smaller cir needle.

Rotate center panel 90° clockwise. Pick up and knit 1 st in side edge of first row, then BO that st, pick up and knit 39 (44, 49, 54, 59, 64, 69) more sts evenly along the selvedge edge of center panel—40 (45, 50, 55, 60, 65, 70) sts.

Working back and forth in rows, knit 2 (4, 8, 12, 16, 20, 24) rows, ending with a RS row.

Shape Neck

INC ROW: (WS) Knit to last st, M1 (see Glossary), k1—1 st inc'd.

Knit 5 (5, 7, 7, 7, 7, 7) rows.

Rep the last 6 (6, 8, 8, 8, 8, 8) rows 1 (4, 2, 4, 4, 5, 5) more time(s)—42 (50, 53, 60, 65, 71, 76) sts.

Sizes 33½ (37½, 40½, 44½, 49)" only

INC ROW: (WS) Knit to last st, M1, k1—1 st inc'd.

Knit 3 (3, 5, 5, 5) rows.

Rep the last 4 (4, 6, 6, 6) rows 5 (2, 2, 0, 0) more times—48 (53, 56, 61, 66) sts.

All sizes

INC ROW: (WS) Knit to last st, M1, k1—49 (54, 57, 62, 67, 72, 77) sts.

Divide sts as evenly as possible on 3 dpn.

NEXT ROW: (RS) Knit to last st, pm—1 st unworked.

Sleeve

JOINING RND: P2tog (unworked st from last row and first st of rnd), purl to end—48 (53, 56, 61, 66, 71, 76) sts rem.

Cont in garter st (alternate knit 1 rnd, purl 1 rnd) for 45 (33, 29, 21, 17, 13, 13) rnds, ending after a knit rnd.

DEC RND: P1, p2tog, purl to last 2 sts, ssp (see Glossary)—2 sts dec'd.

Rep the last 46 (34, 30, 22, 18, 14, 14) rnds 0 (2, 0, 2, 2, 7, 2) more times—46 (47, 54, 55, 60, 55, 70) sts rem.

[Work in garter st for 41 (29, 25, 17, 13, 9, 9) rnds, ending after a knit rnd. Rep dec rnd] 2 (1, 4, 4, 6, 3, 10) time(s)—42 (45, 46, 47, 48, 49, 50) sts rem.

Cont in garter st until piece measures 17¼ (17½, 17¾, 18, 18¼, 18½, 18¾)" [44 (44.5, 45, 45.5, 46.5, 47, 47.5) cm] from joining rnd, ending with a purl rnd.

Using the picot method, BO as foll: BO 1 st, *sl 1 st on right needle tip to left needle tip, use the cable method (see Glossary) to CO 2 sts, BO 4 sts; rep from * to last st, sl st on right needle tip to left needle tip, use the cable method to CO 2 sts, BO 3 sts, pick up and knit 1 st from beg of rnd, BO 1 st. Cut yarn and pull tail through rem st to fasten off.

Right Body

With a single strand of yarn, smaller cir needle, and RS facing, pick up and knit 40 (45, 50, 55, 60, 65, 70) sts evenly spaced along the right edge of center panel.

Knit 2 (4, 8, 12, 16, 20, 24) rows, ending with a RS row.

Shape Neck

INC ROW: (WS) K1, M1, knit to end—1 st inc'd.

Knit 5 (5, 7, 7, 7, 7, 7) rows.

Rep the last 6 (6, 8, 8, 8, 8, 8) rows 1 (4, 2, 4, 4, 5, 5) more time(s)—42 (50, 53, 60, 65, 71, 76) sts.

Sizes 33½ (37½, 40½, 44½, 49)" only
INC ROW: (WS) K1, M1, knit to end—1 st inc'd.

Knit 3 (3, 5, 5, 5) rows.

Rep the last 4 (4, 6, 6, 6) rows 5 (2, 2, 0, 0) more times—48 (53, 56, 61, 66) sts.

All sizes
INC ROW: (WS) K1, M1, knit to end—49 (54, 57, 62, 67, 72, 77) sts.

Divide sts as evenly as possible on 3 dpn.

NEXT ROW: (RS) Knit to last st, pm—1 st unworked.

Sleeve

Work as for left sleeve.

Finishing

Edging

With a single strand of yarn, smaller cir needle, RS facing, and beg at one sleeve join, *pick up and knit 20 (24, 26, 30, 32, 35, 37) sts along body, 28 (28, 30, 30, 32, 32, 34) sts across center panel, 20 (24, 26, 30, 32, 35, 37) sts along body to join on next sleeve; rep from * once—136 (152, 164, 180, 192, 204, 216) sts total. Pm and join for working in rnds. Purl 1 rnd, [knit 1 rnd, purl 1 rnd] 2 times.

Use the picot method to BO all sts as for sleeves.

Weave in loose ends. Block to measurements (see Glossary).

---

picking up stitches along a long section

Picking up a large number of stitches evenly spaced along the edge of a long piece can be challenging. To make this easier, place markers to denote 6 or 8 evenly spaced sections (to assist, fold the piece in half 3 or 4 times). Then divide the total number of stitches to be picked up by the number of sections, adjusting a stitch here or there as necessary to evenly distribute the full number of stitches.

unity  PULLOVER

Worked from the neck down, this simple pullover is a great first-sweater project for cable-lovers. Stitches are increased over a handful of rows spaced throughout the yoke, then they are divided for the sleeves and body. While the body has some basic waist shaping, the sleeves are worked straight to the cuff. Not only a quick-knit, this sweater is super warm.

finished size

About 30¾ (34¼, 37¼, 40½, 44, 46¾, 50¼)" (78 [87, 94.5, 103, 112, 118.5, 127.5] cm) bust circumference.

Pullover shown measures 34¼" (87 cm).

yarn

Chunky weight (#5 Bulky).

SHOWN HERE: Green Mountain Spinnery Yarn Over (predominantly wool with possible alpaca, mohair, or Tencel; 155 yd [142 m]/4 oz): red, 6 (6, 7, 7, 8, 8, 9) skeins.

needles

Size U.S. 10 (6 mm): 16", 24", and 32" (40, 60, and 80 cm) circular (cir) and set of 5 double-pointed (dpn).

Adjust needle size if necessary to obtain the correct gauge.

notions

Cable needle (cn), stitch holder or waste yarn; tapestry needle.

gauge

14 sts and 19 rnds = 4" (10 cm) in St st, worked in rnds.

18 sts and 24 rnds = 4" (10 cm) according to Cable Chart 5, worked in rnds.

STITCH GUIDE

Left Twist (LT): Bring the right needle tip behind the first st on the left needle and knit the second st through the back loop (tbl), keeping both sts on left needle, then knit the first st and slip both sts off the needle tog.

Yoke

With shortest cir needle, use the long-tail method (see Glossary) to CO 54 (57, 60, 63, 63, 66, 69) sts. Being careful not to twist sts, join for working garter st (see Glossary) so that the joining bump is on the RS. Place marker (pm) to denote beg of rnd.

Knit 1 rnd, purl 1 rnd, knit 1 rnd.

Note: Change to longer needles when there are too many sts to fit comfortably on shorter needles.

INC RND 1: P10 (1, 9, 3, 11, 8, 5), M1P (see Glossary), *p4 (4, 3, 3, 2, 2, 2), M1 (see Glossary); rep from *—66 (72, 78, 84, 90, 96, 102) sts.

Knit 1 rnd even.

NEXT RND: *P1, k2; rep from *.

NEXT RND: *K1, LT (see Stitch Guide); rep from *.

INC RND 2: *P1, M1P, k2; rep from *—88 (96, 104, 112, 120, 128, 136) sts.

Beg with Rnd 1, work Cable Chart 1 for 1 (1, 3, 1, 3, 1, 3) rnd(s).

INC RND 3: *P1, M1P, p1, k1, M1, k1; rep from *—132 (144, 156, 168, 180, 192, 204) sts.

Work Cable Chart 2 for 3 rnds.

INC RND 4: *P3, k2, M1, k1; rep from *—154 (168, 182, 196, 210, 224, 238) sts.

Work Cable Chart 3 for 7 (3, 3, 7, 7, 11, 11) rnds.

INC RND 5: *P3, k2, M1, k2; rep from *—176 (192, 208, 224, 240, 256, 272) sts.

Work Cable Chart 4 for 5 (11, 11, 11, 11, 11, 11) rnds.

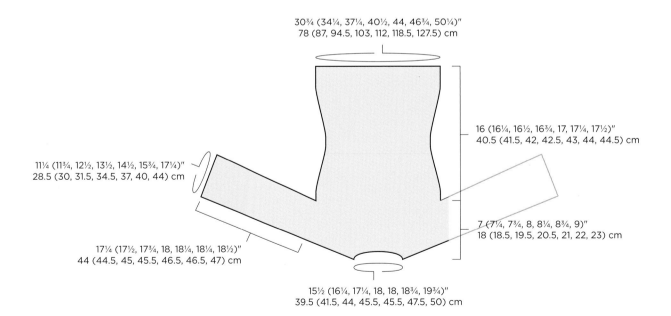

30¾ (34¼, 37¼, 40½, 44, 46¾, 50¼)"
78 (87, 94.5, 103, 112, 118.5, 127.5) cm

16 (16¼, 16½, 16¾, 17, 17¼, 17½)"
40.5 (41.5, 42, 42.5, 43, 44, 44.5) cm

11¼ (11¾, 12½, 13½, 14½, 15¾, 17¼)"
28.5 (30, 31.5, 34.5, 37, 40, 44) cm

7 (7¼, 7¾, 8, 8¼, 8¾, 9)"
18 (18.5, 19.5, 20.5, 21, 22, 23) cm

17¼ (17½, 17¾, 18, 18¼, 18¼, 18½)"
44 (44.5, 45, 45.5, 46.5, 46.5, 47) cm

15½ (16¼, 17¼, 18, 18, 18¾, 19¾)"
39.5 (41.5, 44, 45.5, 45.5, 47.5, 50) cm

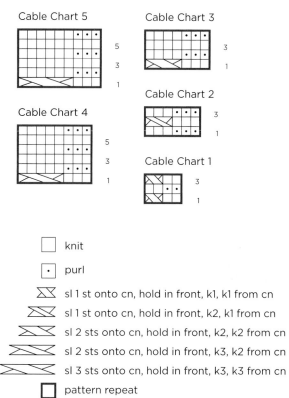

Cable Chart 5

Cable Chart 3

Cable Chart 4

Cable Chart 2

Cable Chart 1

knit

purl

sl 1 st onto cn, hold in front, k1, k1 from cn

sl 1 st onto cn, hold in front, k2, k1 from cn

sl 2 sts onto cn, hold in front, k2, k2 from cn

sl 2 sts onto cn, hold in front, k3, k2 from cn

sl 3 sts onto cn, hold in front, k3, k3 from cn

pattern repeat

INC RND 6: *P3, k3, M1, k2; rep from *—198 (216, 234, 252, 270, 288, 306) sts.

Work Cable Chart 5 for 8 rnds.

DEC RND: K12 (14, 15, 2, 4, 27, 7), ssk, *k6 (6, 5, 6, 6, 5, 7), ssk; rep from *—174 (190, 202, 220, 236, 250, 272) sts rem.

Purl 1 rnd, then knit 4 rnds—piece measures about 7 (7¼, 7¾, 8, 8¼, 8¾, 9)" (18 [18.5, 19.5, 20.5, 21, 22, 23] cm) from CO.

Divide for Sleeves and Body

*K51 (57, 61, 67, 72, 76, 82) for back, place next 36 (38, 40, 43, 46, 49, 54) sts onto holder or waste yarn for sleeve, use the backward-loop method (see Glossary) to CO 1 (1, 2, 2, 2, 3, 3) st(s), pm for side, CO 2 (2, 2, 2, 3, 3, 3) more sts; rep from * once for front and second sleeve—108 (120, 130, 142, 154, 164, 176) sts rem for body; 54 (60, 65, 71, 77, 82, 88) sts each for front and back. Second marker placed is the new beg of rnd.

trying on top-down sweaters and making adjustments

The benefit of working a sweater from the top-down is that it can be tried on as it's being knitted. Although the sweater can be tried on at any point, be sure to try it on a few rounds after the body has been divided for front(s), back, and sleeves. At this point you'll get a good feel for how the yoke fits around the shoulders and underarms.

To try on a sweater in progress, slip all of the stitches and markers onto a length of waste yarn that is long enough to allow all of the stitches to spread out fully. Pull the sweater over your head and evaluate the fit. If you like how it fits, great—keep knitting. If not—you can make one or more of the following adjustments:

If the yoke feels too long or too short: Rip back to before the sleeves and body were divided and adjust the length of the yoke to the desired length. If shortening the yoke, note if any increase or decrease rows were worked in the rounds you don't need, and work them on an earlier round so your stitch count remains the same at the end of the revised yoke.

If the sleeves and body feel too tight or too loose: Typically, stitches are cast on for the underarm at the base of the yoke. If both the body and sleeve stitches feel too tight or too loose, adjust the number of cast-on stitches for a more comfortable fit.

If the body feels too loose and the sleeves feel too tight (or vice versa): Shift the point of the underarm divide until both the body and sleeves feel comfortable. For example, if 120 stitches are too loose for the body and 57 stitches are too tight for the sleeves, try transferring some of the body stitches to the sleeves—perhaps 116 stitches for the body and 59 stitches for the sleeves.

Body

Knit 5 rnds.

DEC RND: *K1, ssk, work to 3 sts before next m, k2tog, k1, sl m; rep from *—4 sts dec'd.

Knit 6 (6, 6, 7, 7, 8, 8) rnds.

Rep the last 7 (7, 7, 8, 8, 9, 9) rnds 2 more times, then work dec rnd once again—92 (104, 114, 126, 138, 148, 160) sts rem.

Knit 5 rnds.

INC RND: *K1, M1, work to 1 st before next m, M1, k1, sl m; rep from *—4 sts inc'd.

Knit 9 rnds.

Rep the last 10 rnds 2 more times, then work inc rnd once again—108 (120, 130, 142, 154, 164, 176) sts.

Cont even in St st until piece measures 15½ (15¾, 16, 16¼, 16½, 16¾, 17)″ (39.5 [40, 40.5, 41.5, 42, 42.5, 43] cm) from dividing rnd.

Purl 1 rnd, then knit 1 rnd.

BO all sts purlwise.

Sleeves

Return 36 (38, 40, 43, 46, 49, 54) held sleeve sts onto 3 dpns. With empty needle, pick up and knit 5 (5, 6, 6, 7, 8, 8) sts from underarm CO sts of body. Pm near center of picked up sts to mark beg of rnd—41 (43, 46, 49, 53, 57, 62) sts total.

DEC RND: Knit to last of the held sts, ssk (1 held st with 1 picked up st), knit to end of rnd, slip marker (sl m), knit to last picked up st, k2tog (1 picked up st with 1 held st)—39 (41, 44, 47, 51, 55, 60) sts rem.

Cont even in St st until piece measures 16¾ (17, 17¼, 17½, 17¾, 17¾, 18)″ (42.5 [43, 44, 44.5, 45, 45, 45.5] cm) from dividing rnd.

Purl 1 rnd, then knit 1 rnd.

BO all sts purlwise.

Finishing

Weave in loose ends. Block to measurements (see Glossary).

divine VEST

Beginning with a provisional cast-on, this vest features unusual construction. The pockets are shaped with short-rows, then the hem is folded to the wrong side and joined to live stitches for the body. After the body and hood are completed, stitches are picked up for the front band while joining the pockets to the body seamlessly. Like the ubiquitous hoodie, this super-comfortable vest is sure to become a daily favorite.

finished size

About 31¼ (34½, 37½, 41, 44¼, 47¾, 51)" (79.5 [87.5, 95, 104, 112.5, 121.5, 129.5] cm) bust circumference, buttoned and including ½" (1.3 cm) overlap.

Vest shown measures 34½" (87.5 cm).

yarn

Worsted weight (#4 Medium).

SHOWN HERE: O-Wool Balance (50% organic cotton, 50% organic wool; 130 yd [119 m]/50 g): #3222 malachite, 7 (8, 9, 9, 10, 11, 12) skeins.

needles

BODY, SLEEVES, AND HOOD: size U.S. 5 (3.75 mm): 32" (80 cm) circular (cir).

EDGINGS: size U.S. 4 (3.5 mm): 16" and 40" (40 and 100 cm) cir.

Adjust needle size if necessary to obtain the correct gauge.

notions

Cable needle (cn); markers (m); waste yarn and size G/6 (4 mm) crochet hook for provisional CO; removable markers; stitch holders or waste yarn; tapestry needle; four 1" (2.5 cm) buttons.

gauge

19 sts and 27 rows = 4" (10 cm) in Rev St st on larger needle.

10 sts of cable panel = 1¼" (3 cm) wide on larger needle.

STITCH GUIDE

Cable Panel: (panel of 10 sts)

ROWS 1, 3, 7, AND 9: (RS) Knit.

ROWS 2, 4, 6, AND 8: Purl.

ROW 5: Sl 5 sts onto cn and hold in front of work, k5, k5 from cn.

ROW 10: Purl.

Rep Rows 1–10 for patt.

NOTES

→ *Vest is worked from the bottom up, beginning with the hem.*

→ *Before joining the facing to the body, the pockets are shaped with short-rows.*

→ *The pockets will hang loose until they are joined with the body when stitches are picked up for the buttonband.*

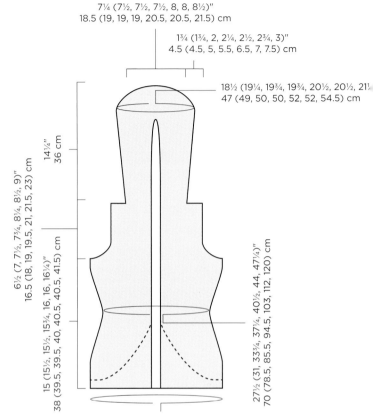

7¼ (7½, 7½, 7½, 8, 8, 8½)"
18.5 (19, 19, 19, 20.5, 20.5, 21.5) cm

1¾ (1¾, 2, 2¼, 2½, 2¾, 3)"
4.5 (4.5, 5, 5.5, 6.5, 7, 7.5) cm

18½ (19¼, 19¾, 19¾, 20½, 20½, 21¼)"
47 (49, 50, 50, 52, 52, 54.5) cm

14¼"
36 cm

6½ (7, 7½, 7¾, 8¼, 8½, 9)"
16.5 (18, 19, 19.5, 21, 21.5, 23) cm

15 (15½, 15½, 15¾, 16, 16, 16¼)"
38 (39.5, 39.5, 40, 40.5, 40.5, 41.5) cm

27½ (31, 33¾, 37¼, 40½, 44, 47¼)"
70 (78.5, 85.5, 94.5, 103, 112, 120) cm

31¾ (35, 38, 41½, 44¾, 48¼, 51½)"
80.5 (89, 96.5, 105.5, 113.5, 122.5, 131) cm

Body

With smaller needle, waste yarn, and crochet hook, use the crochet chain method (see Glossary) to provisionally CO 146 (162, 176, 192, 208, 224, 240) sts. Do not join. Work back and forth in rows as foll:

With working yarn and beg with a RS row, work 9 rows even in St st (knit RS rows; purl WS rows) for facing, ending with a RS row.

TURNING ROW: (WS) With larger cir needle, knit.

Work 8 more rows in St st, ending with a WS row.

Right Pocket

Work short-rows (see Glossary) as foll:

SHORT-ROW 1: With RS facing, k36, wrap next st, turn work so WS is facing, purl to end.

SHORT-ROW 2: With RS facing, knit to 2 sts before previously wrapped st, wrap next st, turn work so WS is facing, purl to end.

Rep Short-Row 2 eight more times.

SHORT-ROW 3: With RS facing, knit to 1 st before wrapped st, wrap next st, turn work so WS is facing, purl to end.

Rep Short-Rows 2 and 3 two more times, then rep Short-Row 3 nine more times.

SHORT-ROW 4: With RS facing, k37 hiding wraps by knitting them tog with their wrapped sts, wrap next st, turn work so WS is facing, purl to end.

NEXT ROW: With RS facing, k37, place marker (pm), knit to end hiding rem wrap as it appears.

picking up stitches with a smaller needle

To prevent picked-up stitches from appearing loose and sloppy, use a needle one or two sizes smaller to pick up the stitches, then work them with the correct-size needle on the first row or round.

Left Pocket

SHORT-ROW 1: With WS facing, p36, wrap next st, turn work so RS is facing, knit to end.

SHORT-ROW 2: With WS facing, purl to 2 sts before previously wrapped st, wrap next st, turn work so RS is facing, knit to end.

Rep Short-Row 2 eight more times.

SHORT-ROW 3: With WS facing, purl to 1 st before wrapped st, wrap next st, turn work so RS is facing, knit to end.

Rep Short-Rows 2 and 3 two more times, then rep Short-Row 3 nine more times.

SHORT-ROW 4: With WS facing, k37 hiding wraps by knitting them tog with their wrapped sts, wrap next st, turn work so RS is facing, knit to end.

NEXT ROW: With WS facing, loosely BO 37 sts knitwise, purl to m, loosely BO rem 37 sts—72 (88, 102, 118, 134, 150, 166) body sts rem. Cut yarn.

Join Hem

Carefully remove waste yarn from provisional CO and place 146 (162, 176, 192, 208, 224, 240) exposed sts onto smaller cir needle. With WS of provisional CO sts facing and beg at edge of right pocket, join yarn and use a second larger cir needle to p37 provisionally CO sts, hold sts from other end of larger cir needle in front of the provisionally CO sts, then k2tog (1 st from each needle) until all sts are joined, p37 rem provisionally CO sts—146 (162, 176, 192, 208, 224, 240) sts.

SET-UP ROW: (WS) K7, pm, p1, [p1, M1P (see Glossary)] 4 times, p1, pm, knit to last 13 sts, pm, p1, [M1P, p1] 4 times, p1, pm, k7—154 (170, 184, 200, 216, 232, 248) sts.

NEXT ROW: (RS) *Work in Rev St st (purl RS rows; knit WS rows) to m, work 10 sts according to Row 1 of cable panel patt (see Stitch Guide); rep from * once more, work in Rev St st to end.

Cont in patt as established until piece measure 3″ (7.5 cm) from turning row, ending with a RS row.

NEXT ROW: (WS) Keeping in patt, work 40 (44, 48, 52, 56, 60, 64) sts for left front, pm for side "seam," work 74 (82, 88, 96, 104, 112, 120) sts for back, pm for other side "seam," work rem 40 (44, 48, 52, 56, 60, 64) sts for right front.

Shape Waist

DEC ROW: (RS) Keeping in patt, *work to 4 sts before side m, ssp (see Glossary), p2, slip marker (sl m), p2, p2tog; rep from * once, work to end—4 sts dec'd.

Work 5 rows even.

Rep the last 6 rows 1 more time—146 (162, 176, 192, 208, 224, 240) sts rem. [Rep dec row, then work 7 rows even] 3 times—134 (150, 164, 180, 196, 212, 228) sts rem; 35 (39, 43, 47, 51, 55, 59) sts for each front; 64 (72, 78, 86, 94, 102, 110) sts for back.

Cont even as established until piece measures 9" (23 cm) from turning row, ending with a WS row.

Shape Bust

INC ROW: (RS) Keeping in patt, *work to 2 sts before side m, M1P, p2, sl m, p2, M1P; rep from * once more, work to end—4 sts inc'd.

Work 7 rows even. Rep the last 8 rows 0 (0, 1, 1, 2, 3, 3) time(s)—138 (154, 172, 188, 208, 228, 244) sts. [Rep inc row, then work 5 rows even] 4 (4, 3, 3, 2, 1, 1) time(s)—154 (170, 184, 200, 216, 232, 248) sts; 40 (44, 48, 52, 56, 60, 64) sts for each front; 74 (82, 88, 96, 104, 112, 120) sts for back.

Cont even as established until piece measures 15 (15½, 15½, 15¾, 16, 16, 16¼)" (38 [39.5, 39.5, 40, 40.5, 40.5, 41.5] cm) from turning row, ending with a WS row.

Divide for Armholes

With RS facing, *work to 3 (3, 4, 4, 5, 5, 5) sts before side m, BO 6 (6, 8, 8, 10, 10, 10) sts removing m when you come to it; rep from * once more, work to end—37 (41, 44, 48, 51, 55, 59) sts rem for each front; 68 (76, 80, 88, 94, 102, 110) sts rem for back.

Cont working back and forth on 37 (41, 44, 48, 51, 55, 59) left front sts only; place sts for right front and back onto holders, waste yarn, or leave on cir needle to be worked later.

Left Front

Work 1 WS row even as established.

Shape Armhole

DEC ROW: (RS) Keeping in patt, p1, p2tog, work to end—1 st dec'd.

Work 1 WS row even. Rep the last 2 rows 4 (8, 8, 12, 13, 17, 19) more times—32 (32, 35, 35, 37, 37, 39) sts rem. [Rep dec row, then work 3 rows even] 4 (3, 4, 2, 2, 1, 1) time(s)—28 (29, 31, 33, 35, 36, 38) sts rem.

Cont even as est until armhole measures 6½ (7, 7½, 7¾, 8¼, 8½, 9)" (16.5 [18, 19, 19.5, 21, 21.5, 23] cm), ending with a RS row.

Place all sts onto holder or waste yarn. Do not cut yarn. Set aside.

Back

Return 68 (76, 80, 88, 94, 102, 110) back sts to larger needle in they are not already there and join yarn in preparation to work a WS row. Work 1 WS row even.

Shape Armholes

DEC ROW: (RS) P1, p2tog, work to last 3 sts, ssp, p1—2 sts dec'd.

Work 1 WS row even. Rep the last 2 rows 4 (8, 8, 12, 13, 17, 19) more times—58 (58, 62, 62, 66, 66, 70) sts rem. [Rep dec row, then work 3 rows even] 4 (3, 4, 2, 2, 1, 1) time(s)—50 (52, 54, 58, 62, 64, 68) sts rem.

Cont even as established until armholes measure 6½ (7, 7½, 7¾, 8¼, 8½, 9)" (16.5 [18, 19, 19.5, 21, 21.5, 23] cm), ending with a RS row.

Join Left Shoulder

Keeping 9 (9, 10, 12, 13, 14, 15) sts at left armhole edge of back on larger cir needle, place rem 41 (43, 44, 46, 49, 50, 53) sts onto holder or waste yarn. Place 8 (8, 9, 11, 12, 13, 14) sts from armhole edge of left front onto a second needle. With RS facing tog, use the three-needle method (see Glossary) to BO 8 (8, 9, 11, 12, 13, 14) shoulder sts tog (when binding off the last st, only 1 st rem on back and no sts rem on front), slip rem st from BO onto same holder as back sts—20 (21, 22, 22, 23, 23, 24) sts rem for left front; 42 (44, 45, 47, 50, 51, 54) sts rem for back.

Right Front

Return 37 (41, 44, 48, 51, 55, 59) right front sts onto larger needle, if they are not already there, and join yarn in preparation to work a WS row.

Work 1 WS row even as established.

Shape Armhole

DEC ROW: (RS) Work to last 3 sts, ssp, p1—1 st dec'd.

Work 1 WS row even. Rep the last 2 rows 4 (8, 8, 12, 13, 17, 19) more times—32 (32, 35, 35, 37, 37, 39) sts rem. [Rep dec row, then work 3 rows even] 4 (3, 4, 2, 2, 1, 1) time(s)—28 (29, 31, 33, 35, 36, 38) sts rem.

Cont even as established until armhole measures 6½ (7, 7½, 7¾, 8¼, 8½, 9)" (16.5 [18, 19, 19.5, 21, 21.5, 23] cm), ending with a RS row.

Join Right Shoulder

Keeping 8 (8, 9, 11, 12, 13, 14) sts at armhole edge of right front on larger cir needle, place rem 20 (21, 22, 22, 23, 23, 24) sts onto holder or waste yarn. Place 9 (9, 10, 12, 13, 14, 15) sts from right armhole edge of back onto a second needle. With RS facing tog, use the three-needle method to BO 8 (8, 9, 11, 12, 13, 14) shoulder sts tog (when binding off the last st, only 1 st rem on back and no sts rem on front), slip rem st from BO onto same holder as back sts—20 (21, 22, 22, 23, 23, 24) sts rem for each front; 34 (36, 36, 36, 38, 38, 40) sts rem for back.

Hood

Place all held front and back sts onto larger cir needle—74 (78, 80, 80, 84, 84, 88) sts total. Cont working with yarn attached to left front as foll:

DEC ROW: (WS) Keeping in patt, work 19 (20, 21, 21, 22, 22, 23) sts, sl 1 knitwise with yarn in front (kwise wyf), pick up and knit 1 st from gap at BO and put it onto the left needle tip, k3tog, psso, work 30 (32, 32, 32, 34, 34, 36) sts, sl 1 kwise wyf, sl 1 purlwise with yarn in front (pwise wyf), pick up and knit 1 st from gap at BO and put it onto the left needle tip, return 1 slipped st from right needle tip to left needle tip, k3tog, psso, work to end—70 (74, 76, 76, 80, 80, 84) sts rem.

Cont even as established until piece measures 1" (2.5 cm) from dec row, ending with a RS row.

SET-UP ROW: (WS) Keeping in patt, work 26 (27, 28, 28, 29, 29, 30) sts, pm, work 18 (20, 20, 20, 22, 22, 24) sts, pm, work to end.

INC ROW: (RS) Work to m, M1P, sl m, work to next m, sl m, M1P, work to end—2 sts inc'd.

Work 5 rows even.

Rep the last 6 rows 12 times—96 (100, 102, 102, 106, 106, 110) sts. Remove markers. Cont as established until hood measures about 13" (33 cm) from shoulders, ending with WS Row 2 of cable patt.

Shape Top

Pm each side of center 8 sts.

DEC ROW: (RS) Keeping in patt, work to first m, sl m, p2tog, work to 2 sts before next m, ssp, sl m, work to end—2 sts dec'd.

Work 1 WS row even.

Rep the last 2 rows 3 more times—88 (92, 94, 94, 98, 98, 102) sts rem.

Divide sts evenly onto 2 needles, hold the needles parallel with RS of hood facing tog and use the three-needle method to BO all sts tog.

Finishing

Align pockets along front edges of body and use removable markers to pin in place, being sure that both pockets are of equal heights.

Place 4 removable markers along the right front edge for buttonhole placement, the first at the top of the pocket and the rem 3 markers 2" (5 cm) above the previously placed marker.

Front Band

With RS facing, smaller cir needle, and beg at lower right front edge, pick up and knit 369 (379, 384, 390, 395, 400, 408) sts evenly spaced to lower left front edge, picking up through both body and pocket layers and picking up about 3 sts for every 4 rows. Knit 3 rows.

BUTTONHOLE ROW: (RS) *Knit to buttonhole m, work one-row buttonhole over 3 sts (see Glossary); rep from * 3 more times, knit to end.

With WS facing, BO all sts knitwise.

Armhole Edging

With RS facing and smaller 16" (40 cm) cir needle, pick up and knit 74 (80, 87, 89, 96, 99, 104) sts (about 3 sts for every 4 rows and 1 st for each BO underarm st) evenly spaced around armhole opening. Pm and join for working in rnds. Purl 1 rnd, then knit 1 rnd.

BO all sts purlwise.

Weave in loose ends. Block to measurements (see Glossary).

Sew buttons to left front opposite buttonholes.

whisper  TUNIC

Knitted with two strands of linen yarn held together, Whisper is an elegant warm-weather cardigan. It easily adapts to a variety of styles—over a simple dress for a splash of lacey class or as a simple cover-up while wandering the beach. Knitted from the bottom up, it is shaped by changing to progressive needle sizes along the way. The sleeves and neck are shaped without interrupting the lace pattern. Easy!

finished size

About 31¼ (35, 38¾, 42½, 46¼, 50, 53¾)" (79.5 [89, 98.5, 108, 117.5, 127, 136.5] cm) bust circumference, buttoned with 1" (2.5 cm) overlap.

Tunic shown measures 35" (89 cm).

yarn

Sportweight (#2 Fine).

SHOWN HERE: Louet Euroflax (100% linen; 270 yd [246 m]/100 g): #68 steel grey, 7 (8, 8, 9, 10, 11, 12) skeins.

needles

BODY AND SLEEVES: sizes U.S. 10 (6 mm) and 11 (8 mm): 32" (80 cm) circular (cir) each.

EDGINGS: size U.S. 6 (4 mm): 16" (40 cm) and 32" (80 cm) cir.

Adjust needle size if necessary to obtain the correct gauge.

notions

Cable needle (cn); stitch holders or waste yarn; markers (m); five 1" (2.5 cm) buttons.

gauge

20 sts (2 patt reps) and 28 rows (1 patt rep) = 3¾" (9.5 cm) wide and 3½" (9 cm) tall in charted patt on smallest needles with 2 strands of yarn held tog.

20 sts (2 patt reps) and 28 rows (1 patt rep) = 4½" (11.5 cm) wide and 6¼" (16 cm) tall in charted patt on medium-size needles with 2 strands of yarn held tog.

20 sts (2 patt reps) and 28 rows (1 patt rep) = 5¾" (14.5 cm) wide and 9" (23 cm) tall in charted patt on largest needles with 2 strands of yarn held tog.

13 sts and 9 rows = 4" (10 cm) wide and 1" (2.5 cm) tall in garter st on smallest needles with 2 strands of yarn held tog.

Body

With smallest needle and 2 strands of yarn held tog, use the long-tail method (see Glossary) to CO 162 (182, 202, 222, 242, 262, 282) sts. Do not join. Knit 2 rows.

Change to largest needles and work Rows 1–28 of Cathedral Lace chart, then work Rows 1–14 once more.

Change to medium needle and work Rows 15–28 of chart, then work Rows 1–28 once more.

Change to smallest needle and work Rows 1–13 of chart—piece measures about 24¾" (63 cm) from CO.

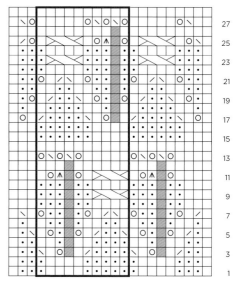

Cathedral Lace

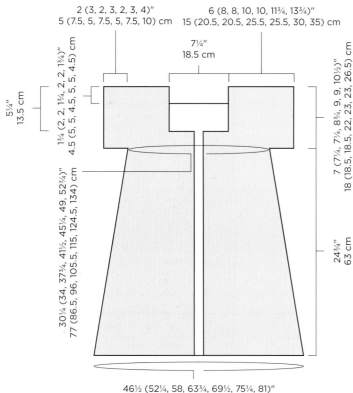

2 (3, 2, 3, 2, 3, 4)"
5 (7.5, 5, 7.5, 5, 7.5, 10) cm

6 (8, 8, 10, 10, 11¾, 13¾)"
15 (20.5, 20.5, 25.5, 25.5, 30, 35) cm

7¼"
18.5 cm

5¼"
13.5 cm

1¾ (2, 2, 1¾, 2, 2, 1¾)"
4.5 (5, 5, 4.5, 5, 5, 4.5) cm

7 (7¼, 7¼, 8¾, 9, 9, 10½)"
18 (18.5, 18.5, 22, 23, 23, 26.5) cm

30¼ (34, 37¾, 41½, 45¼, 49, 52¾)"
77 (86.5, 96, 105.5, 115, 124.5, 134) cm

24¾"
63 cm

46½ (52¼, 58, 63¾, 69½, 75¼, 81)"
118 (132.5, 147.5, 162, 176.5, 191, 205.5) cm

☐ knit on RS; purl on WS

• purl on RS; knit on WS

O yo

╱ k2tog

╲ ssk

⋀ s2kp

⤬ sl 2 sts onto cn and hold in front of work, k2, k2 from cn

▨ no stitch

☐ pattern repeat

Divide for Sleeves

With WS facing and keeping in patt, work 41 (46, 51, 56, 61, 66, 71) sts, then place these sts onto holder or waste yarn for left front, work 80 (90, 100, 110, 120, 130, 140) sts for back, then place rem 41 (46, 51, 56, 61, 66, 71) sts onto holder or waste yarn for right front—80 (90, 100, 110, 120, 130, 140) sts rem for back.

Back

Use the cable method (see Glossary) to CO 11 (16, 11, 16, 11, 16, 21) sts at beg of next 2 rows—102 (122, 122, 142, 142, 162, 182) sts.

Keeping in patt, work 40 (40, 40, 54, 54, 54, 68) more rows, ending with WS Row 28 (28, 28, 14, 14, 14, 28) of chart.

Shape Neck

With RS facing, work 32 (42, 42, 52, 52, 62, 72) sts, join 2 more strands of yarn and BO center 38 sts, work to end—32 (42, 42, 52, 52, 62, 72) sts rem each side. Working each side separately and keeping in patt, work 13 (15, 15, 13, 15, 15, 13) rows, ending with WS Row 14 (16, 16, 28, 2, 2, 14) of chart. Place sts onto holders or waste yarn. Cut yarn.

Left Front

Return 41 (46, 51, 56, 61, 66, 71) held left front sts to smaller needle in preparation to work a RS row.

NEXT ROW: (RS) With RS of back facing, hold garment upside down with sleeve CO sts at the top, and beg at cuff edge, pick up and knit 11 (16, 11, 16, 11, 16, 21) sts along CO sts of back sleeve (see sidebar on page 94), work as charted to end—52 (62, 62, 72, 72, 82, 92) sts.

Work 12 (14, 14, 26, 28, 28, 40) rows in patt, ending with RS Row 27 (1, 1, 13, 15, 15, 27) of chart.

Shape Neck

With WS facing, BO 20 sts, work to end—32 (42, 42, 52, 52, 62, 72) sts rem.

Cont in patt for 42 rows, ending with WS Row 14 (16, 16, 28, 2, 2, 14) of chart.

Join Left Shoulder

Return 32 (42, 42, 52, 52, 62, 72) held left back sts onto empty tip of smaller needle. Hold needles parallel with RS of knitting facing tog and use the three-needle method (see Glossary) to BO sts tog.

Right Front

Return 41 (46, 51, 56, 61, 66, 71) held right front sts onto smaller needle and join 2 strands of yarn in preparation to work a WS row. Work 1 WS row as even as charted.

NEXT ROW: (RS) Keeping in patt, work to end of row, then with RS of back facing, hold garment with sleeve CO sts at the top, and beg at body edge, pick up and knit 11 (16, 11, 16, 11, 16, 21) sts along the CO sts—52 (62, 62, 72, 72, 82, 92) sts total.

Work 13 (15, 15, 27, 29, 29, 41) rows even in patt, ending with WS Row 28 (2, 2, 14, 16, 16, 28) of chart.

Shape Neck

With RS facing, BO 20 sts, work to end—32 (42, 42, 52, 52, 62, 72) sts rem.

Cont in patt for 41 rows, ending with WS row 14 (16, 16, 28, 2, 2, 14) of chart.

Join Right Shoulder

Return 32 (42, 42, 52, 52, 62, 72) held right back sts onto empty tip of smaller needle. Hold needles parallel with RS of knitting facing tog and use the three-needle method to BO sts tog.

Finishing

Weave in loose ends. Block to measurements (see Glossary).

Sleeve Edging

With smallest 16″ (40 cm) cir needle, RS facing, and holding 2 strands of yarn tog, pick up and knit 52 (54, 54, 66, 68, 68, 78) sts evenly spaced around sleeve edge. Pm and join for working in rnds. [Purl 1 rnd, knit 1 rnd] 4 times—4 garter ridges on RS. BO all sts purlwise.

Neckband

With smallest 32″ (80 cm) cir needle, RS facing, 2 strands of yarn held tog, and beg at right front neck edge, pick up and knit 15 sts across front neck BO, pm, 26 sts along right neck edge, pm, 28 sts across back neck BO, pm, 26 sts along left neck edge, pm then pick up and knit 15 sts along left front neck BO—110 sts total.

Purl 1 WS row.

DEC ROW: (RS) Knit to 2 sts before m, k2tog, sl m, ssk; rep from * 3 more times, knit to end—8 sts dec'd.

Rep the last 2 rows 3 more times—78 sts rem.

BO all sts knitwise.

Buttonband

With smallest 32" (80 cm) cir needle, RS facing, 2 strands of yarn held tog, and beg at neck edge of left front, pick up and knit 85 (86, 86, 91, 92, 92, 97) sts evenly spaced along front edge. Knit 8 rows, ending with a RS row—4 garter ridges on RS. BO all sts knitwise.

Buttonhole Band

With smallest 32" (80 cm) cir needle, RS facing, 2 strands of yarn held tog, and beg at lower edge of right front, pick up and knit 85 (86, 86, 91, 92, 92, 97) sts evenly spaced along front edge. Knit 3 rows, ending with a WS row.

BUTTONHOLE ROW: (RS) K22 (23, 23, 24, 25, 25, 26), BO 3 sts, *k11 (11, 11, 12, 12, 12, 13), BO 3 sts; rep from * 3 more times, k4 to end—5 buttonholes made.

NEXT ROW: (WS) *Knit to BO sts, use the cable method to CO 3 sts; rep from * 4 more times to complete buttonholes, knit to end.

Knit 3 rows even. BO all sts knitwise.

Sew buttons to buttonband, opposite buttonholes.

hope  TOP

Designed for seed-stitch lovers (like me), Hope can be worn alone or over a fitted blouse, with a skirt or jeans. It is worked from the top down with beautiful details along the way, including a dainty button closure at the back neck, prominent slipped stitches along the yoke, and a drawstring waist. Knitted in a blend of linen and merino at a fine gauge, this sweater is a joy both to knit and wear.

finished size

About 30¾ (34½, 38½, 42¼, 46¼, 50¼, 54)" (78 [87.5, 98, 107.5, 117.5, 127.5, 137] cm) bust circumference.
Top shown measures 34½" (87.5 cm).

yarn

Sportweight (#2 Fine).

SHOWN HERE: Louet MerLin (60% linen, 40% merino; 250 yd [228 m]/ 100 g): #67 sea foam green, 3 (4, 4, 5, 5, 6, 6) skeins.

needles

BODY AND SLEEVES: size U.S. 1 (2.25 mm): 16" and 32" (40 and 80 cm) circular (cir) and set of 4 or 5 double-pointed (dpn).

I-CORD: size U.S. 0 (2 mm): set of 2 double-pointed (dpn).

Adjust needle size if necessary to obtain the correct gauge.

notions

Markers (m); stitch holders or waste yarn; one ½" (1.3 cm) button; tapestry needle.

gauge

24 sts and 46 rnds = 4" (10 cm) in seed st on larger needle, worked in rnds.

25 sts and 52 rnds = 4" (10 cm) in slipped seed st on larger needle, worked in rnds.

Seed Stitch Worked in Rows: (multiple of 2 sts)

ROW 1: (WS) *P1, k1; rep from *.

ROW 2: (RS) *K1, p1; rep from *.

Rep Rows 1 and 2 for patt.

Seed Stitch Worked in Rounds: (multiple of 2 sts + 1)

RND 1: K1, *p1, k1; rep from *.

RND 2: P1, *k1, p1; rep from *.

Rep Rnds 1 and 2 for patt.

Slipped Seed Stitch: (multiple of 6 sts + 5)

RND 1: P1, k1, sl 1 purlwise with yarn in back (pwise wyb), k1, p1, *k1, p1, k1, sl 1 pwise wyb, k1, p1; rep from *.

RND 2: K1, p1, sl 1 pwise wyb, p1, k1, *p1, k1, p1, sl 1 pwise wyb, p1, k1; rep from *.

RND 3: P1, k1, knit next st wrapping yarn twice, k1, p1, *k1, p1, k1, knit next st wrapping yarn twice, k1, p1; rep from *.

RND 4: Rep Rnd 2, dropping extra wraps.

Rep Rnds 1–4 for patt.

NOTES

→ Garment is worked from the top down.

→ When counting sts, count each double yarnover as 1 stitch.

Yoke

With shorter cir needle, use the long-tail method (see Glossary) to CO 92 (100, 108, 116, 124, 132, 140) sts. Do not join; work back and forth in rows.

Work 2 rows in seed st (see Stitch Guide).

BUTTON-LOOP ROW: (WS) Use the knitted method (see Glossary) to CO 1 st, [CO 1 st, BO 1 st] 8 times, k2tog, work to end in seed st as established—92 (100, 108, 116, 124, 132, 140) sts.

Work 7 rows even in seed st, ending with a RS row. Do not turn.

JOINING RND: With RS still facing, spread sts along needle and form work into a ring being careful not to twist sts as foll: Sl first st with yarn in back (wyb), work in seed st to last st, then knit the last and first sts tog as k2tog, pm for beg of rnd—91 (99, 107, 115, 123, 131, 139) sts rem.

INC RND 1: (P1, [yo] 2 times, p1) all in next st, *k1, (p1, [yo] 2 times, p1) all in next st; rep from *—183 (199, 215, 231, 247, 263, 279) sts, counting each double yo as 1 st.

Establish slipped seed st as foll:

RND 1: K1, sl 1 purlwise with yarn in back (pwise wyb) while dropping extra wrap, k1, *p1, k1, sl 1 pwise wyb while dropping extra wrap, k1; rep from *.

RND 2: P1, sl 1 pwise wyb, p1, *k1, p1, sl 1 pwise wyb, p1; rep from *.

RND 3: K1, sl 1 pwise wyb, k1, *p1, k1, sl 1 pwise wyb, k1; rep from *.

RND 4: P1, knit next st wrapping yarn twice, p1, *k1, p1, knit next st wrapping yarn twice, p1; rep from *.

Rep these 4 rnds 7 (7, 8, 8, 9, 9, 10) more times, then work Rnds 1–3 once again—piece measures about 3¾ (3¾, 4, 4, 4¼, 4¼, 4½)" (9.5 [9.5, 10, 10, 11, 11, 11.5] cm) from CO.

INC RND 2: P1, yo, knit next st wrapping yarn twice, yo, p1, *k1, p1, yo, knit next st wrapping yarn twice, yo, p1; rep from *—275 (299, 323, 347, 371, 395, 419) sts.

NEXT RND: K1, p1 through back loop (p1tbl), sl 1 pwise wyb while dropping extra wrap, p1tbl, k1, *p1, k1, p1tbl, sl 1 pwise wyb while dropping extra wrap, p1tbl, k1; rep from *.

Work Rnds 1–4 of slipped seed st 12 (13, 13, 14, 14, 15, 15) times, then work Rnds 1 and 2 once again.

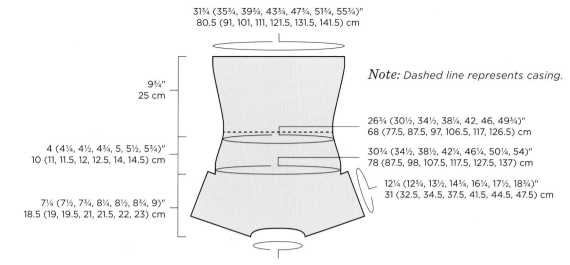

31¾ (35¾, 39¾, 43¾, 47¾, 51¾, 55¾)"
80.5 (91, 101, 111, 121.5, 131.5, 141.5) cm

9¾"
25 cm

Note: Dashed line represents casing.

26¾ (30½, 34½, 38¼, 42, 46, 49¾)"
68 (77.5, 87.5, 97, 106.5, 117, 126.5) cm

4 (4¼, 4½, 4¾, 5, 5½, 5¾)"
10 (11, 11.5, 12, 12.5, 14, 14.5) cm

30¾ (34½, 38½, 42¼, 46¼, 50¼, 54)"
78 (87.5, 98, 107.5, 117.5, 127.5, 137) cm

12¼ (12¾, 13½, 14¾, 16¼, 17½, 18¾)"
31 (32.5, 34.5, 37.5, 41.5, 44.5, 47.5) cm

7¼ (7½, 7¾, 8¼, 8½, 8¾, 9)"
18.5 (19, 19.5, 21, 21.5, 22, 23) cm

15¼ (16¾, 18, 19¼, 20¾, 22, 23¼)"
38.5 (42.5, 45.5, 49, 52.5, 56, 59) cm

Divide for Armholes

Keeping in patt, work 41 (46, 51, 55, 59, 63, 67) sts for right back, place next 56 (58, 60, 64, 68, 72, 76) sts onto holder or waste yarn for sleeve, turn work so WS is facing and use the cable method (see Glossary) to CO 14 (16, 18, 22, 26, 30, 34) sts, turn work so RS is facing, work 81 (91, 101, 109, 117, 125, 133) sts for front, place next 56 (58, 60, 64, 68, 72, 76) sts onto holder or waste yarn for other sleeve, turn work so WS is facing and use the cable method to CO 14 (16, 18, 22, 26, 30, 34) sts, turn work so RS is facing, work rem 41 (46, 51, 55, 59, 63, 67) sts for left back—191 (215, 239, 263, 287, 311, 335) sts rem; 41 (46, 51, 55, 59, 63, 67) sts for each back, 81 (91, 101, 109, 117, 125, 133) sts for front, 14 (16, 18, 22, 26, 30, 34) sts for each underarm.

Body

Working back and front sts in patt as established and working underarm sts in seed sts, work even for 10 (10, 14, 14, 18, 18, 22) rnds, ending with Rnd 2 of patt.

Shape Waist

Note: The decreases are worked on the 2 seed sts closest to the last slipped st of the slipped seed patt.

DEC RND: Work Rnd 3 of patt to last slipped st before underarm seed sts, knit the next st, wrapping yarn twice, k2tog, work in seed st to 2 sts before next slipped st, ssk; rep from * once more, work to end in patt—4 sts dec'd.

Work 7 rnds even in patt.

Rep the last 8 rnds 2 (3, 3, 4, 4, 5, 5) more times—179 (199, 223, 243, 267, 287, 311) sts rem.

Cont for your size as foll.

Sizes 30¾ (34½, 38½, 42¼, 46¼)" only
Rep dec rnd, then work 3 rnds even. Rep the last 4 rnds 2 (1, 1, 0, 0) time(s)—167 (191, 215, 239, 263) sts rem.

All sizes
Work 4 rnds even, then purl 1 rnd—piece measures 4 (4¼, 4½, 4¾, 5, 5½, 5¾)" (10 [11, 11.5, 12, 12.5, 14, 14.5] cm) from underarm CO.

Waist Casing

Knit 2 rnds.

EYELET RND: [Yo] 2 times, k2tog, knit to end.

NEXT RND: Knit yo while dropping extra wrap, knit to end.

NEXT RND: K1 in the row below the st on the needle, knit to end.

Knit 1 rnd.

JOINING RND: (see box at right) *With left needle tip, lift back of st from 6 rows below and knit it tog with the next st on needle; rep from *.

Purl 1 rnd.

SET-UP RND: Work 79 (91, 103, 115, 127, 139, 151) sts in seed st, place marker (pm), knit next st wrapping yarn twice, p7, knit next st wrapping yarn twice, pm, work rem 79 (91, 103, 115, 127, 139, 151) sts in seed st.

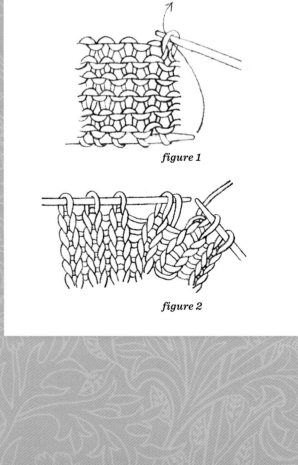

how to join a casing

A small casing for an I-cord tie is worked at the waist of this sweater. Six rounds of stockinette stitch form the casing. The casing is joined into a tube on the next round when the stitches on the needle are worked together with the loops on the wrong side of the stitches 6 rounds below as follows:

Joining rnd: *Bring the yarn to the front of the work to get it out of the way, then fold the left needle toward you so you can see the wrong side of the work. Beginning with the stitch on the needle, insert the left needle tip into the back of corresponding stitch 6 rows below the stitch on the needle (**Figure 1**), then bring the yarn to the back and knit this loop together with the first stitch on the needle as k2tog (**Figure 2**) to join the 2 rows. Repeat from * to the end of the round.

figure 1

figure 2

NEXT RND: Work in seed st to m, slip marker (sl m), sl 1 pwise wyb while dropping extra wrap, purl to 1 st before next m, sl 1 pwise wyb while dropping extra wrap, sl m, work in seed st to end.

Work 2 rnds in patt as established.

Shape Hips

RND 1: (inc rnd) Work in seed st to m, sl m, knit next st wrapping yarn twice, M1P (see Glossary), purl to 1 st before next m, M1P, knit next st wrapping yarn twice, sl m, work in seed st to end—2 sts inc'd.

RND 2: Work in seed st to m, sl m, sl 1 pwise wyb while dropping extra wrap, purl to 1 st before next m, sl 1 pwise wyb while dropping extra wrap, sl m, work in seed st to end.

RNDS 3 and 4: Work in seed st to m, sl m, sl 1 pwise wyb, purl to 1 st before next m, sl 1 pwise wyb, sl m, work in seed st to end.

RND 5: Work in seed st to m, sl m, knit next st wrapping yarn twice, purl to 1 st before next m, knit next st wrapping yarn twice, sl m, work in seed st to end.

RNDS 6–12: Rep Rnds 2–5 once, then rep Rnds 2–4 once more.

Rep these 12 rnds 2 more times—173 (197, 221, 245, 269, 293, 317) sts.

NEXT RND: (inc rnd) Work 20 (22, 24, 28, 30, 34, 36) sts in seed st, (k1, yo, k1) all in next st, work in seed st to m, sl m, knit next st wrapping yarn twice, M1P, purl to 1 st before next m, M1P, knit next st wrapping yarn twice, sl m, work in seed st to last 21 (23, 25, 29, 31, 35, 37) sts, (k1, yo, k1) all in next st, work in seed st to end—179 (203, 227, 251, 275, 299, 323) sts.

Rep Rnds 2–12 once, then work Rnds 1–12 three times—185 (209, 233, 257, 281, 305, 329) sts.

NEXT RND: (inc rnd) Work 22 (24, 26, 30, 32, 36, 38) sts in seed st, (k1, yo, k1) all into next st, work in seed st to m, sl m, knit next st wrapping yarn twice, M1P, purl to 1 st before next m, M1P, knit next st wrapping yarn twice, sl m, work in seed st to last 23 (25, 27, 31, 37, 39) sts, (k1, yo, k1) all into next st, work in seed st to end—191 (215, 239, 263, 287, 311, 335) sts.

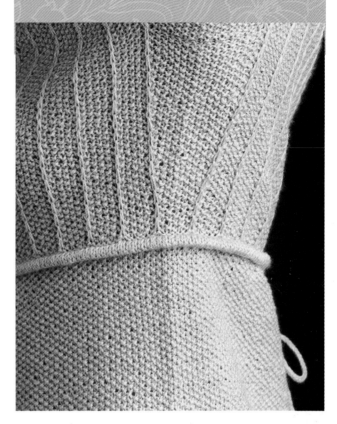

Rep Rnds 2–12 once.

Work 11 rnds even in seed st. BO all sts in patt.

Sleeves

Place 56 (58, 60, 64, 68, 72, 76) held sleeve sts onto larger dpns, join yarn with RS facing, and pick up and knit 18 (20, 22, 26, 30, 34, 38) sts along underarm CO sts—74 (78, 82, 90, 98, 106, 114) sts total. Pm and join for working in rnds.

DEC RND: Work in seed st to last 2 sts, k2tog or p2tog as necessary to maintain patt—73 (77, 81, 89, 97, 105, 113) sts rem.

Work 7 rnds even in seed st. Loosely BO all sts in patt.

Finishing

Weave in loose ends. Block to measurements (see Glossary).

Cord

With smaller dpn and leaving a long tail about 4" (10 cm) long to help pull cord through casing, CO 2 sts. Work 2 st I-cord (see Glossary) until piece measures 58 (62, 66, 70, 74, 78, 82)" (147.5 [157.5, 167.5, 178, 188, 198, 208.5] cm) from CO.

NEXT ROW: K2tog.

Cut yarn and draw tail through rem st to fasten off.

Thread long CO tail onto tapestry needle and tie a knot just below eye of needle, leaving enough to weave in after threading cord through the casing. Carefully pull cord through casing. Weave in loose ends. Tie ends into a bow.

With yarn threaded on a tapestry needle, sew button opposite button loop.

honor ❦ PULLOVER

Beginning with stitches cast on for the outer edge of the collar, short-rows are used to shape the ribbed collar and V-neck as stitches are increased along raglan lines for the yoke of this flirty pullover. The body and sleeves are worked in rounds to the lower edges. A bit of waist shaping and elongated ribs add style to this wear-everywhere pullover.

finished size

About 33½ (36½, 40½, 43½, 47½, 50½, 54)" (85 [92.5, 103, 110.5, 120.5, 128.5, 137] cm) bust circumference

Pullover shown measures 36½" (92.5 cm).

yarn

Worsted weight (#4 Medium).

SHOWN HERE: Fibre Company Organik (70% organic merino, 15% alpaca, 15% silk; 98 yd [89 m]/50 g): coral reef, 10 (11, 12, 13, 14, 15, 16) skeins.

needles

Size U.S. 8 (5 mm): 16" and 32" (40 and 80 cm) circular (cir) and set of 4 or 5 double-pointed (dpn).

Adjust needle size if necessary to obtain the correct gauge.

notions

Markers (m); stitch holders or waste yarn; tapestry needle.

gauge

16 sts and 25 rows or rnds = 4" (10 cm) in St st.

Body

With longer cir needle, use the long-tail method (see Glossary) to CO 182 (189, 196, 203, 210, 217, 224) sts. Do not join; work back and forth in rows as foll.

Collar

ROW 1: (RS) Purl.

ROW 2: (WS) [K1, M1 (see Glossary)] 2 times, knit to last 2 sts, [M1, k1] 2 times—186 (193, 200, 207, 214, 221, 228) sts.

ROW 3: (RS) Rep Row 2, but do not turn the work at end of row—190 (197, 204, 211, 218, 225, 232) sts.

Being careful not to twist sts, join for working in rnds by spreading sts out along needle and with RS facing, slip first st from left needle tip to right needle tip, bring yarn from back to front between needles and return slipped st to left needle tip. Turn work and place marker (pm) for beg of rnd.

Establish rib pattern and work short-rows (see Glossary) as foll, changing to shorter cir needle when sts no longer fit comfortably on longer cir needle:

SHORT-ROW 1: (WS) P3, k2, *p5, k2; rep from * last 3 sts, p1, wrap next st, turn work.

SHORT-ROW 2: (RS) K1, p2, *ssk, k1, k2tog, p2; rep from * to last 3 sts, k1, wrap next st, turn work—138 (143, 148, 153, 158, 163, 168) sts rem.

SHORT-ROW 3: P1, k2, *p3, k2; rep from * to 1 st before wrapped st, wrap next st, turn work.

SHORT-ROW 4: P2, sl 1, k2tog, psso work in rib to 6 sts before wrapped st, sl 1, k2tog, psso, p2, wrap next st, turn work—134 (139, 144, 149, 154, 159, 164) sts rem.

SHORT-ROW 5: Work in rib to 3 sts before wrap, wrap next st, turn work.

Pm each side of center 12 (17, 22, 27, 22, 27, 22) sts.

SHORT-ROW 6: P2, sl 1, k2tog, psso, work in rib to 2 sts before m, ssk or ssp (see Glossary) as necessary to maintain patt, slip marker (sl m), p2, *k3, p2; rep from * to next m, sl m, k2tog or p2tog as necessary to maintain patt, work rib as established to 8 sts before wrapped st, sl 1, k2tog, psso, p2, wrap next st, turn work—6 sts dec'd.

SHORT-ROW 7: Work in rib to 3 sts before wrapped st, wrap next st, turn work.

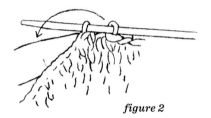

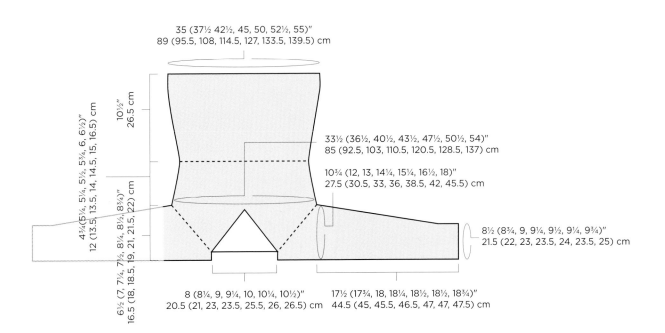

35 (37½ 42½, 45, 50, 52½, 55)"
89 (95.5, 108, 114.5, 127, 133.5, 139.5) cm

10½"
26.5 cm

33½ (36½, 40½, 43½, 47½, 50½, 54)"
85 (92.5, 103, 110.5, 120.5, 128.5, 137) cm

10¾ (12, 13, 14¼, 15¼, 16½, 18)"
27.5 (30.5, 33, 36, 38.5, 42, 45.5) cm

4¾ (5¼, 5½, 5¾, 6, 6½)"
12 (13.5, 13.5, 14, 14.5, 15, 16.5) cm

8½ (8¾, 9, 9¼, 9½, 9¼, 9¾)"
21.5 (22, 23, 23.5, 24, 23.5, 25) cm

6½ (7, 7¼, 7½, 8¼, 8½, 8¾)"
16.5 (18, 18.5, 19, 21, 21.5, 22) cm

8 (8¼, 9, 9¼, 10, 10¼, 10½)"
20.5 (21, 23, 23.5, 25.5, 26, 26.5) cm

17½ (17¾, 18, 18¼, 18½, 18½, 18¾)"
44.5 (45, 45.5, 46.5, 47, 47, 47.5) cm

SHORT-ROW 8: P2, sl 1, k2tog, psso, work in rib to 8 sts before wrapped st, sl 1, k2tog, psso, p2, wrap next st, turn work—4 sts dec'd.

SHORT-ROW 9: Work in rib to 3 sts before wrapped st, wrap next st, turn work.

Rep Short-rows 6–9 four more times—84 (89, 94, 99, 104, 109, 114) sts rem.

Cont for your size as foll.

Sizes 47½ (50½, 54)" only

Rep Short-rows 8 and 9 one (one, two) more time(s)—100 (105, 106) sts rem.

All sizes

NEXT ROW: P2, [sl 1, k2tog, psso, p2] 2 (3, 4, 5, 4, 5, 4) time(s), wrap next st, turn work—80 (83, 86, 89, 92, 95, 98) sts rem.

Remove markers. Cut yarn. Slip sts as necessary so that needle tips are at beg of rnd.

With RS facing, rejoin yarn and work as foll, hiding wraps as they appear:

Note: Back neck sts are BO, then picked up to maintain the stability of the neck.

K16 (17, 18, 19, 20, 21, 22), pm, k8 (8, 7, 7, 6, 6, 6), pm, BO 32 (33, 36, 37, 40, 41, 42) sts, sl last st from right needle tip to left needle, cut yarn, rejoin yarn at the first BO st, then pick up and knit 32 (33, 36, 37, 40, 41, 42) sts evenly spaced across the BO edge, pm, sl 1 pwise wyb, k7 (7, 6, 6, 5, 5, 5), pm, k16 (17, 18, 19, 20, 21, 22), wrap the first st of the rnd, turn work.

Yoke

Note: The RS of the collar becomes the WS of the yoke. Neck shaping is introduced while raglan shaping is in progress; read all the way through the foll section before proceeding.

NEXT SHORT-ROW: (RS) Knit to last m, sl m, k2, wrap next st, turn work.

NEXT SHORT-ROW: Purl to last m, sl m, p2, wrap next st, turn work.

INC ROW: (RS) *Knit to 1 st before m, M1R (see Glossary), k1, sl m, k1, M1L (see Glossary); rep from * 3 more times, knit to wrapped st, knit wrap tog with wrapped st, wrap next st, turn work—88 (91, 94, 97, 100, 103, 106) sts.

Cont for your size as foll, changing to longer cir needle when necessary:

Sizes 33½ (36½)″ only

NEXT ROW: (WS) Purl to wrapped st, purl wrap tog with wrapped st, wrap next st, turn work.

NEXT ROW: Knit to wrapped st, knit wrap tog with wrapped st, wrap next st, turn work.

All sizes

NEXT ROW: (WS) Purl to wrapped st, purl wrap tog with wrapped st, wrap next st, turn work.

INC ROW 1: (RS) *Knit to 1 st before m, M1R, k1, sl m, k1, M1L; rep from * 3 more times, knit to wrapped st, knit wrap tog with wrapped st, wrap next st, turn work—8 sts inc'd.

Rep the last 2 rows 10 (11, 13, 14, 15, 16, 17) more times, then work WS row once more.

INC ROW 2: (RS) *Knit to 1 st before m, M1R, k1, sl m, k1, M1L; rep from * 3 more times, knit to end, working wrap tog with wrapped st—184 (195, 214, 225, 236, 247, 258) sts; 29 (31, 34, 36, 38, 40, 42) sts for each front, 34 (36, 39, 41, 42, 44, 46) sts for each sleeve, 58 (61, 68, 71, 76, 79, 82) sts for back.

Continue working in rnds for your size as foll.

Sizes 33½ (40½, 47½)″ only

Knit 1 rnd.

Sizes 36½ (43½, 50½)″ only

DEC RND: Knit to last 2 sts, ssk—194 (224, 246) sts rem; 61 (71, 79) sts each for front and back, 36 (41, 44) sts for each sleeve.

Size 54″ only:

DEC RND: K2tog, knit to last 2 sts, ssk—256 sts rem; 82 sts each for front and back, 46 sts for each sleeve.

All sizes

INC RND: *Knit to 1 st before m, M1R, k1, sl m, k1, M1L; rep from * 3 more times, knit to end—8 sts inc'd.

Knit 1 rnd even.

Rep the last 2 rnds 1 (2, 2, 1, 2, 1, 0) more time(s)—200 (218, 238, 240, 260, 262, 264) sts. Rep inc rnd 1 (1, 1, 3, 3, 5, 7) more time(s)—208 (226, 246, 264, 284, 302, 320) sts; 64 (69, 76, 81, 88, 93, 98) sts each for front and back, 40 (44, 47, 51, 54, 58, 62) sts for each sleeve.

Divide for Lower Body and Sleeves

Remove beg-of-rnd m, knit to first raglan m, remove m, place next 40 (44, 47, 51, 54, 58, 62) sts onto holder or waste yarn for sleeve, remove next m, use the backward-loop method (see Glossary) to CO 1 (2, 2, 3, 3, 4, 5) st(s), pm for new beg of rnd, CO 2 (2, 3, 3, 4, 4, 5) more sts, work 64 (69, 76, 81, 88, 93, 98) back sts, remove m, place next 40 (44, 47, 51, 54, 58, 62) sts onto holder or waste yarn for sleeve, remove m, use the backward-loop method to CO 1 (2, 2, 3, 3, 4, 5) st(s), pm for side "seam," CO 2 (2, 3, 3, 4, 4, 5) more sts, knit to end of rnd—134 (146, 162, 174, 190, 202, 216) sts rem for body.

Knit every rnd until piece measures 1″ (2.5 cm) from dividing rnd.

Shape Waist

DEC RND: *K0 (1, 0, 1, 0, 1, 1), k2tog, knit to 3 sts before next m, ssk, k1; rep from * once more—4 sts dec'd.

Knit 4 (5, 5, 6, 6, 7, 8) rnds even.

Rep the last 5 (6, 6, 7, 7, 8, 9) rnds 2 more times, then work dec rnd again—118 (130, 146, 158, 174, 186, 200) sts rem. Knit 3 (2, 3, 2, 3, 2, 2) rnds, then purl 2 (3, 2, 2, 2, 2, 3) rnds.

Cont for your size as foll.

Sizes 33½ (40½, 43½, 47½, 50½)″ only

INC RND: *P29 (25, 39, 21, 31), [M1P (see Glossary), p30 (24, 40, 22, 31)] 1 (2, 1, 3, 2) time(s), sl m; rep from * once more—120 (150, 160, 180, 190) sts.

Sizes 36½ (54)″ only

Increases are complete.

All sizes

Piece measures about 4¾ (5¼, 5¼, 5½, 5¾, 6, 6½)" [12 (13.5, 13.5, 14, 14.5, 15, 16.5) cm] from underarm CO.

Knit 1 rnd.

SET-UP PATT: [K1, p3, *k2, p3; rep from * to 1 st before m, k1, sl m] 2 times.

Work even in rib as established for 9 more rnds.

INC RND: *K1, M1 or M1P as necessary to maintain patt, work as established to 1 st before m, M1 or M1P as necessary to maintain patt, k1; rep from * once more—4 sts inc'd.

Work 9 rnds even in rib as established. Rep the last 10 rnds 4 more times—140 (150, 170, 180, 200, 210, 220) sts.

Knit 1 rnd. Purl 3 rnds—piece measures about 15¼ (15¾, 15¾, 16, 16¼, 16½, 17)" [38.5 (40, 40, 40.5, 41.5, 42, 43) cm] from underarm CO. BO all sts purlwise.

Sleeves

With dpn, RS facing, and beg at center of underarm CO sts, pick up and knit 3 (3, 4, 4, 5, 5, 6) sts, k40 (44, 47, 51, 54, 58, 62) held sleeve sts, then pick up and knit 2 (3, 3, 4, 4, 5, 6) sts from rem underarm CO sts—45 (50, 54, 59, 63, 68, 74) sts total. Pm for beg of rnd.

DEC RND 1: K2 (2, 3, 3, 4, 4, 5), k2tog, knit to last 3 (4, 4, 5, 5, 6, 7) sts, ssk, k1 (2, 2, 3, 3, 4, 5)—43 (48, 52, 57, 61, 66, 72) sts rem.

Knit 8 rnds even.

DEC RND 2: K1, k2tog, knit to last 3 sts, ssk, k1—41 (46, 50, 55, 59, 64, 70) sts rem.

Knit 9 rnds. Purl 2 (2, 3, 3, 2, 2, 3) rnds.

Cont for your size as foll.

Sizes 33½ (36½)" only

P1, p2tog, purl to end—40 (45) sts rem.

Sizes 40½ (54)" only

Shaping is complete.

Sizes 47½ (50½)" only

P1, M1P, purl to end—60 (65) sts.

All sizes

Knit 1 rnd.

SET-UP RND: K1, p3, k1; rep from *.

Work even as established for 23 (15, 11, 9, 7, 5, 5) more rnds.

DEC RND: K1, p2tog or k2tog as necessary to maintain patt, work to last 3 sts, ssp or ssk as necessary to maintain patt, k1—2 sts dec'd.

Rep the last 24 (16, 12, 10, 8, 6, 6) rnds 2 (1, 1, 1, 4, 9, 6) more time(s)—34 (41, 46, 51, 50, 45, 56) sts rem.

Cont for your size as foll.

Size 33½″ only

Shaping is complete.

Sizes 36½ (40½, 43½, 47½, 50½, 54)″ only

Work 13 (9, 7, 5, 3, 3) rnds even.

DEC RND: K1, p2tog or k2tog as necessary to maintain patt, work to last 3 sts, ssp or ssk as necessary to maintain patt, k1—2 sts dec'd.

Rep the last 14 (10, 8, 6, 4, 4) rnds 2 (4, 6, 5, 3, 8) more times—35 (36, 37, 38, 37, 38) sts rem.

All sizes

Cont in rib as established until piece measures 16¾ (17, 17¼, 17½, 17¾, 17¾, 18)″ (42.5 [43, 44, 44.5, 45, 45, 45.5] cm) from pick-up rnd.

Knit 1 rnd, then purl 3 rnds.

BO all sts purlwise.

Finishing

Weave in loose ends. Block to measurements (see Glossary).

delight  PULLOVER

This cozy pullover is ideal for super-chilly mid-winter days. It's a beautifully warm sweater that begins with the largest needle and progresses through smaller needles to draw in at the waist. The sleeve stitches are provisionally cast on, then the fronts and back are worked separately while the sleeve caps and neck are shaped. For minimal fuss, the sleeves and shoulders are joined with a three-needle bind-off.

finished size

About 32 (35¼, 38¾, 42, 45½, 48¾, 52¼)" (81.5 [89.5, 98.5, 106.5, 115.5, 124, 132.5] cm) bust circumference.
Pullover shown measures 35¼" (89.5 cm).

yarn

Bulky weight (#6 Super Bulky).

SHOWN HERE: Spud & Chloë Outer (65% superwash wool, 35% organic cotton; 60 yd [55 m]/100 g): #7203 carbon, 10 (11, 11, 12, 13, 14, 15) skeins.

needles

BODY AND SLEEVES: sizes U.S. 15, 13, and 11 (10, 9, and 8 mm): 32" (80 cm) circular (cir) each.

PLACKET AND SLEEVE EDGING: size U.S. 11 (8 mm): set of 4 double-pointed (dpn).

Adjust needle size if necessary to obtain the correct gauge.

notions

Markers (m); stitch holders or waste yarn; size L/11 (8 mm) crochet hook and waste yarn for provisional cast on; tapestry needle.

gauge

12 sts and 16 rnds = 4" (10 cm) in garter cross rib patt on smallest needles, worked in rnds.

9½ sts and 14½ rnds = 4" (10 cm) in St st on smallest needles, worked in rnds.

Body

With largest cir needle, use the long-tail method (see Glossary) to CO 96 (104, 112, 120, 128, 136, 144) sts. Being careful not to twist sts, join for working garter st (see Glossary) so that the joining bump is on the RS. Place marker (pm) to denote beg of rnd. Work Rnds 1–10 of Garter Cross Rib chart. Change to middle-size cir needle and work Rnds 1–10 two times. Change to smallest cir needle and work Rnds 1–10, then work Rnds 1–9 once again—piece measures about 11½" (29 cm) from CO.

DEC RND: *K2, p1, drop 1 st off needle to front, sl 2 purlwise with yarn in back (pwise wyb), drop 1 st off needle to front, use left needle tip to pick up first dropped st, return 2 sl sts to left needle, pick up second dropped st, ssk, k2tog, p1; rep from *—72 (78, 84, 90, 96, 102, 108) sts rem.

Purl 1 rnd. [Knit 1 rnd. Purl 1 rnd] 2 times.

Divide for Front Split

Cut yarn. Remove m, sl 24 (24, 24, 30, 30, 30, 30) sts purlwise, pm to denote new beg of rnd.

Cont for your size as foll.

Size 32" only

NEXT ROW: (RS) With an empty dpn, pick up and knit 4 sts from behind the last 4 slipped sts, working into the garter ridge 2 rows below, keep the slipped sts on dpn (these sts will be worked at the beg of RS rows and the end of WS rows; keep working sts on dpns until they can comfortably fit onto cir needle), k16, pm for side "seam," k36, pm for other side "seam," k20 to end—76 sts; 20 sts for each front; 36 sts for back.

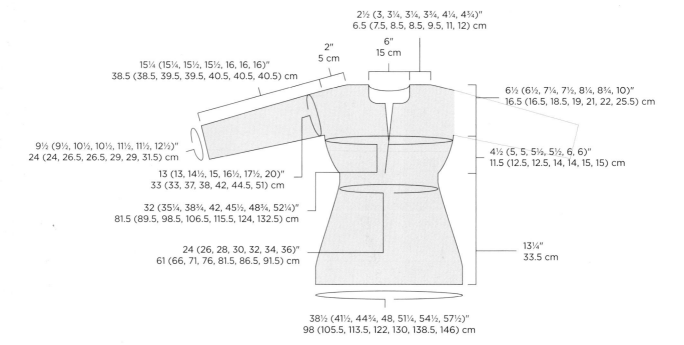

2½ (3, 3¼, 3¼, 3¾, 4¼, 4¾)"
6.5 (7.5, 8.5, 8.5, 9.5, 11, 12) cm

2"
5 cm

6"
15 cm

15¼ (15¼, 15½, 15½, 16, 16, 16)"
38.5 (38.5, 39.5, 39.5, 40.5, 40.5, 40.5) cm

6½ (6½, 7¼, 7½, 8¼, 8¾, 10)"
16.5 (16.5, 18.5, 19, 21, 22, 25.5) cm

9½ (9½, 10½, 10½, 11½, 11½, 12½)"
24 (24, 26.5, 26.5, 29, 29, 31.5) cm

4½ (5, 5, 5½, 5½, 6, 6)"
11.5 (12.5, 12.5, 14, 14, 15, 15) cm

13 (13, 14½, 15, 16½, 17½, 20)"
33 (33, 37, 38, 42, 44.5, 51) cm

32 (35¼, 38¾, 42, 45½, 48¾, 52¼)"
81.5 (89.5, 98.5, 106.5, 115.5, 124, 132.5) cm

13¼"
33.5 cm

24 (26, 28, 30, 32, 34, 36)"
61 (66, 71, 76, 81.5, 86.5, 91.5) cm

38½ (41½, 44¾, 48, 51¼, 54½, 57½)"
98 (105.5, 113.5, 122, 130, 138.5, 146) cm

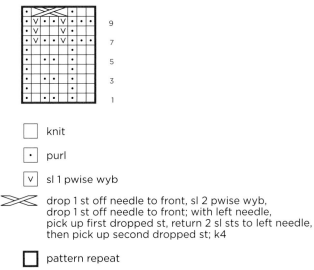

☐ knit

• purl

v sl 1 pwise wyb

⧓ drop 1 st off needle to front, sl 2 pwise wyb,
drop 1 st off needle to front; with left needle,
pick up first dropped st, return 2 sl sts to left needle,
then pick up second dropped st; k4

☐ pattern repeat

Sizes 35¼ (38¾, 42, 45½, 48¾, 52¼)" only

INC ROW: (RS) With an empty dpn, pick up and knit 4 sts from behind the last 4 slipped sts, working into the garter ridge 2 rows below, keep the slipped sts on dpn (these sts will be worked at the beg of RS rows and the end of WS rows; keep working sts on dpns until they can comfortably fit onto cir needle), k18 (10, 10, 8, 8, 7), [M1 (see Glossary), k0 (9, 11, 7, 8, 6)] 0 (1, 1, 2, 2, 3) time(s), pm for side "seam," k10 (11, 10, 9, 5, 7), [M1, k18 (20, 8, 10, 8, 8)] 1 (1, 3, 3, 5, 5) time(s), M1, k10 (11, 10, 9, 5, 7), pm for other side "seam," [k0 (9, 11, 7, 8, 6), M1] 0 (1, 1, 2, 2, 3) time(s), k22 (14, 14, 12, 12, 11) to end—84 (92, 100, 108, 116, 124) sts; 22 (24, 26, 28, 30, 32) sts for each front; 40 (44, 48, 52, 56, 60) sts for back.

All sizes

SET-UP ROW: (WS) Work 4 sts in garter st (knit every row), work in St st (knit RS rows; purl WS rows) to last 4 sts, work 4 sts in garter st.

Shape Placket

DEC ROW: (RS) K4, k2tog, knit to last 6 sts, ssk, k4—2 sts dec'd.

Work 5 (5, 5, 7, 7, 7, 7) rows even as established.

Rep the last 6 (6, 6, 8, 8, 8, 8) rows 0 (1, 1, 0, 0, 1, 1) time—74 (80, 88, 98, 106, 112, 120) sts rem.

shaping sleeve caps for sleeves knitted side to side

Sleeves that are worked simultaneously with the body by casting on the full length of the sleeve at the base of the armholes (**Figure 1**) tend to stretch over the shoulders or pucker at the underarms (**Figure 2**). This can be prevented if extra fabric is added to the tops of the sleeves to accommodate the curve of shoulders.

To do this, place markers on each side of the desired upper body width (aligned with each shoulder). Then, if working from the bottom up, work increases on the stitches outside each marker between the underarms and shoulders (**Figure 3**). If working from the top down, substitute decreases for the increases.

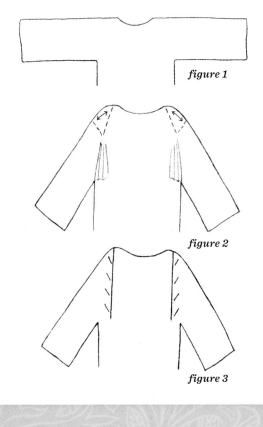

figure 1

figure 2

figure 3

Cont for your size as foll.

Sizes 32 (42, 45½)" only

Rep dec row—72 (96, 104) sts rem. Work 3 (5, 5) rows even as established.

All sizes

Rep dec row, then work 1 WS row even—70 (78, 86, 94, 102, 110, 118) sts rem; 17 (19, 21, 23, 25, 27, 29) sts for each front; 36 (40, 44, 48, 52, 56, 60) sts for back.

NEXT ROW: (RS) Knit to 1 st before m, LT (see Stitch Guide) and replace m in center of these 2 sts, knit to 1 st before next m, RT (see Stitch Guide) and replace m in center of these 2 sts, knit to end (the LT and RT are worked to prevent gaps at the underarms).

Work 1 WS row even—piece measures about 17¾ (18¼, 18¼, 18¾, 18¾, 19¼, 19¼)" (45 [46.5, 46.5, 47.5, 47.5, 49, 49] cm) from CO. Place 17 (19, 21, 23, 25, 27, 29) right front and 36 (40, 44, 48, 52, 56, 60) back sts onto separate holders or waste yarn. Do not cut yarn.

Left Front

With straight needle, crochet hook, and waste yarn, use the crochet provisional method (see Glossary) to CO 36 (36, 37, 37, 38, 38, 38) sts for the left sleeve. With cir needle tip closest to front neck edge of 17 (19, 21, 23, 25, 27, 29) left front sts and a new ball of yarn, k36 (36, 37, 37, 38, 38, 38) newly CO sts, then with RS facing and beg at underarm, work left front sts as established—53 (55, 58, 60, 63, 65, 67) sts total.

Taper Sleeve

Work short-rows (see Glossary) as foll:

SHORT-ROW 1: With WS facing, k4, p25 (27, 30, 29, 30, 30, 30), wrap next st, turn work so RS is facing, knit to last 6 sts, ssk, k4—52 (54, 57, 59, 62, 64, 66) sts rem.

SHORT-ROW 2: With WS facing, k4, p36 (39, 41, 37, 38, 36, 36), wrap next st, turn work so RS is facing, knit to end.

SHORT-ROW 3: With WS facing, k4, p48 (50, 53, 46, 48, 44, 43), wrap next st, turn work so RS is facing, knit to end.

Cont for your size as foll.

Sizes 32 (35¼, 38¾)" only

Short-rows are complete.

Sizes 42 (45½, 48¾, 52¼)" only

SHORT-ROW 4: With WS facing, k4, p55 (58, 52, 50), wrap next st, turn work so RS is facing, knit to end.

Sizes 48¾ (52¼)" only

SHORT-ROW 5: With WS facing, k4, p60 (56), wrap next st, turn work so RS is facing, knit to end.

Size 52¼" only

SHORT-ROW 6: With WS facing, k4, p62, turn work so RS is facing, knit to end.

Shape Sleeve Cap

SET-UP ROW: (RS) K41 (42, 44, 46, 48, 49, 50), M1L (see Glossary), pm, knit to end—53 (55, 58, 60, 63, 65, 67) sts.

Work 1 row even as established.

INC ROW: (RS) Knit to m, M1L, slip marker (sl m), knit to end—1 st inc'd.

Rep the last 2 rows 3 more times—57 (59, 62, 64, 67, 69, 71) sts. Remove m.

Shape Neck

NEXT ROW: (WS) K4, place these 4 sts onto st holder or waste yarn, purl to end—53 (55, 58, 60, 63, 65, 67) sts rem.

DEC ROW: (RS) Knit to last 2 sts, ssk—52 (54, 57, 59, 62, 64, 66) sts rem.

Work 6 (6, 8, 8, 10, 10, 12) rows even in St st, ending with a RS row.

Place sts onto a holder or waste yarn. Cut yarn and set aside.

Back

With straight needle, crochet hook, and waste yarn, use the crochet provisional method to CO 36 (36, 37, 37, 38, 38, 38) sts for right sleeve. Return 36 (40, 44, 48, 52, 56, 60) held back sts to cir needle. With the cir needle tip that is at the left underarm, join new yarn, k36 (36, 37, 37, 38, 38, 38) newly CO sts, then with the RS facing and beg at right underarm, knit the back sts. Beg at left sleeve cuff edge, carefully remove waste yarn from provisional CO and place exposed sts onto left needle tip, k12 (12, 13, 10, 9, 7, 5) newly exposed sts, wrap next st, turn work—108 (112, 118, 122, 128, 132, 136) sts total; 36 (40, 44, 48, 52, 56, 60) back sts, 36 (36, 37, 37, 38, 38, 38) sts for each sleeve.

Taper Sleeves

SHORT-ROW 1: With WS facing, p60 (64, 70, 68, 70, 70, 70), wrap next st, turn work so RS is facing, k72 (76, 82, 77, 79, 77, 77), wrap next st, turn work.

SHORT-ROW 2: With WS facing, p84 (88, 94, 86, 88, 84, 84), wrap next st, turn work so RS is facing, k96 (100, 106, 95, 98, 92, 91), wrap next st, turn work.

SHORT-ROW 3: With WS facing, p108 (112, 118, 104, 108, 100, 98), wrap next st, turn work.

Cont for your size as foll.

Sizes 32 (35¼, 38¾)″ only
Short-rows are complete.

Sizes 42 (45½, 48¾, 52¼)″ only
SHORT-ROW 4: With RS facing, k113 (118, 108, 105), wrap next st, turn work so WS is facing, p122 (128, 116, 112), wrap next st, turn work.

Sizes 48¾ (52¼)″ only
SHORT-ROW 5: With RS facing, k124 (118), wrap next st, turn work so WS is facing, p132 (124) wrap next st, turn work.

Size 52¼″ only
SHORT-ROW 6: With RS facing, k130, turn work so WS is facing, purl to end.

Shape Sleeve Caps

SET-UP ROW: (RS) K41 (42, 44, 46, 48, 49, 50), M1L, pm, k26 (28, 30, 30, 32, 34, 36), pm, M1R (see Glossary), knit to end—110 (114, 120, 124, 130, 134, 138) sts.

Purl 1 WS row.

INC ROW: (RS) Knit to m, M1L, sl m, knit to next m, sl m, M1R, knit to end—2 sts inc'd.

Rep the last 2 rows 3 more times—118 (122, 128, 132, 138, 142, 146) sts. Remove markers. Work 2 (2, 4, 4, 6, 6, 8) rows even in St st, ending with a RS row.

Shape Neck

SET-UP ROW: (WS) P53 (55, 58, 60, 63, 65, 67), pm, p12, pm, purl to end.

NEXT ROW: Knit to m, remove m, join a second ball of yarn, BO center 12 sts and remove second m, knit to end—53 (55, 58, 60, 63, 65, 67) sts rem each side.

DEC ROW: (WS) Purl to 2 sts before BO gap, p2tog; on other side, ssp, purl to end—52 (54, 57, 59, 62, 64, 66) sts rem each side.

Working each side separately, work 3 rows even, ending with a RS row.

Join Left Shoulder

Place right back sts onto waste yarn holder. Cut yarn.

Return 52 (54, 57, 59, 62, 64, 66) held left front sts onto straight needle, fold sleeve so RS are facing tog and WS face outward, then use the three-needle method (see Glossary), to BO all sts.

Right Front

Return 17 (19, 21, 23, 25, 27, 29) held right front sts and 36 (36, 37, 37, 38, 38, 38) provisionally CO sts from back right sleeve to cir needle—53 (55, 58, 60, 63, 65, 67) sts total.

Taper Sleeve

SHORT-ROW 1: With RS facing and the yarn already attached, work 17 (19, 21, 23, 25, 27, 29) right front sts, k12 (12, 13, 10, 9, 7, 5) provisionally CO sts, wrap next st, turn work so WS is facing, purl to last 4 sts, k4.

SHORT-ROW 2: With RS facing, k4, k2tog, k36 (39, 41, 37, 38, 36, 36), wrap next st, turn work so WS is facing, purl to last 4 sts, k4—52 (54, 57, 59, 62, 64, 66) sts rem.

SHORT-ROW 3: With RS facing, k52 (54, 57, 50, 48, 47), wrap next st if you are not at the end of the row, turn work so WS is facing, purl to last 4 sts, k4.

Cont for your size as foll.

Sizes 32 (35¼, 38¾)" only
Short-rows are complete.

Sizes 42 (45½, 48¾, 52¼)" only
SHORT-ROW 4: With RS facing, k59 (62, 56, 54), wrap next st if you are not at the end of the row, turn work so WS is facing, purl to last 4 sts, k4.

Sizes 48¾ (52¼)" only
SHORT-ROW 5: With RS facing, k64 (60), wrap next st if you are not at the end of the row, turn work so WS is facing, purl to last 4 sts, k4.

Size 52¼" only
SHORT-ROW 6: With RS facing, knit to end of row, turn work so WS is facing, purl to last 4 sts, k4.

Shape Sleeve Caps

SET-UP ROW: (RS) K11 (12, 13, 13, 14, 15, 16), pm, M1R, knit to end—53 (55, 58, 60, 63, 65, 67) sts.

Work 1 WS row even.

INC ROW: (RS) Knit to m, sl m, M1R, knit to end—1 st inc'd.

Rep the last 2 rows 3 more times—57 (59, 62, 64, 67, 69, 71) sts. Remove m. Work 1 WS row even.

Shape Neck

DEC ROW: (RS) Sl 4 sts pwise wyb, k2tog, knit to end—56 (58, 61, 63, 66, 68, 70) sts rem.

NEXT ROW: (WS) Purl to last 4 sts, sl last 4 unworked sts onto holder or waste yarn—52 (54, 57, 59, 62, 64, 66) sts rem.

Work 5 (5, 7, 7, 9, 9, 11) rows even in St st, ending with a RS row.

Join Right Shoulder

Place 52 (54, 57, 59, 62, 64, 66) held right back sts onto a second needle, fold sleeve so RS are facing tog and WS face outward, then use the three-needle method to BO all sts.

Finishing

Weave in loose ends. Block to measurements (see Glossary).

Neck Trim

With smallest needle and RS facing, hold yarn in back and sl 4 held right front neck sts. Knit these 4 sts, then pick up and knit 12 (12, 13, 13, 15, 15, 16) sts along back neck edge, 12 sts across back neck, 12 (12, 13, 13, 15, 15, 16) sts to held left front sts, sl 4 held front sts onto empty end of needle, then knit them—44 (44, 46, 46, 50, 50, 52) sts total. Knit 2 rows, ending with a RS row.

With WS facing, BO all sts knitwise.

Cuffs

With dpn and RS facing, pick up and knit 24 (24, 26, 26, 28, 28, 30) sts evenly spaced around sleeve cuff edge. Pm and join for working in rnds. [Purl 1 rnd. Knit 1 rnd] 2 times. BO all sts purlwise.

calm ✿ TEE

The body of this comfortable pullover is worked in one piece from the lower edge to the underarms, at which point the front stitches are placed onto holders while stitches are cast on for the back sleeves and worked with the back in a single piece to the shoulders. Stitches for the front sleeves are then picked up and worked with the front to the shoulders. For a cool-weather variation, simply cast on more stitches for longer sleeves.

finished size
About 30¾ (34½, 38½, 42¼, 46, 50, 53¾)″ (78 [87.5, 98, 107.5, 117, 127, 136.5] cm) bust circumference.
Tee shown measures 34½″ (87.5 cm).

yarn
Sportweight (#2 Fine).

SHOWN HERE: Blue Sky Alpacas Skinny Dyed (100% organic cotton; 150 yd [137 m]/65 g): #318 blackberry, 6 (6, 7, 8, 9, 10, 11) skeins.

needles
Size U.S. 6 (4 mm): 16″ and 32″ (40 and 80 cm) circular (cir) and set of 4 double-pointed (dpn).

Adjust needle size if necessary to obtain the correct gauge.

notions
Stitch holder or waste yarn; markers (m); tapestry needle.

gauge
24 sts and 30 rnds = 4″ (10 cm) in twisted 1x4 rib, worked in rnds.

25 sts and 30 rnds = 4″ (10 cm) according to Leaf chart, worked in rnds.

23 sts and 30 rows = 4″ (10 cm) in Rev St st.

Body

With longer cir needle, use the long-tail method (see Glossary) to CO 180 (200, 220, 240, 260, 280, 300) sts. Place marker (pm) and join for working in rnds, being careful not to twist sts.

Work in twisted 1x1 rib (see Stitch Guide) for 6 rnds.

Work in twisted 1x4 rib (see Stitch Guide) until piece measures 2″ (5 cm) from CO.

Shape Waist

SET-UP RND: Keeping in patt as established, work 90 (100, 110, 120, 130, 140, 150) sts, pm to denote side "seam," work to end of rnd.

DEC RND 1: *K1tbl, p2tog, work in patt to 2 sts before m, ssp (see Glossary), slip marker (sl m); rep from *—4 sts dec'd.

Work 11 (11, 11, 9, 9, 9, 7) rnds even in patt.

Rep the last 12 (12, 12, 10, 10, 10, 8) rnds 2 times—168 (188, 208, 228, 248, 268, 288) sts rem.

DEC RND 2: *K1tbl, sl 1 pwise, sl 1 pwise tbl, return slipped sts to left needle tip and work them as k2tog, work in patt to 2 sts before m, sl 1 pwise tbl, sl 1 kwise, return slipped sts to left needle tip and work them as k2togtbl, sl m; rep from *—164 (184, 204, 224, 244, 264, 284) sts rem.

Work 11 (11, 11, 9, 9, 9, 7) rnds even in patt.

DEC RND 3: *K1tbl, p2tog, work in patt to 2 sts before m, ssp, sl m; rep from *—160 (180, 200, 220, 240, 260, 280) sts rem.

Work 3 (5, 7, 7, 7, 9, 9) rnds even in patt and remove side seam m.

Work set-up rnd of Leaf chart—192 (216, 240, 264, 288, 312, 336) sts.

Work Rnds 1–18 of chart 2 (2, 2, 2, 2, 2, 3) times, then work Rnds 1–9 0 (0, 0, 1, 1, 1, 0) more time.

NEXT RND: P96 (108, 120, 132, 144, 156, 168), pm for underarm, purl to end.

DIVIDING RND: *Work in Rev St st (purl RS rows; knit WS rows) to m, M1 (see Glossary), sl m; rep from *—194 (218, 242, 266, 290, 314, 338) sts.

Place the first 97 (109, 121, 133, 145, 157, 169) onto holder or waste yarn to be worked later for front—97 (109, 121, 133, 145, 157, 169) sts rem for back.

Back

Cont working back sts in Rev St st in rows as foll:

Beg with a WS row, use the cable method (see Glossary) to CO 9 (9, 10, 11, 11, 12, 12) sts at beg of next 2 rows—115 (127, 141, 155, 167, 181, 193) sts.

Work 3 rows even in Rev St st, ending after a WS row.

Shape Sleeve Caps

SET-UP ROW: (RS) P26 (30, 35, 39, 43, 48, 52), pm, p63 (67, 71, 77, 81, 85, 89), pm, purl to end.

INC ROW: (WS) Knit to 1 st before m, M1L (see Glossary), k1, sl m, knit to next m, sl m, k1, M1R (see Glossary), knit to end—2 sts inc'd.

Purl 1 RS row.

Rep the last 2 rows 2 (2, 2, 3, 3, 3, 3) more times—121 (133, 147, 163, 175, 189, 201) sts.

[Rep inc row, work 3 rows even in Rev St st] 7 (7, 8, 8, 9, 9, 10) times—135 (147, 163, 179, 193, 207, 221) sts.

Cont in Rev St st until piece measures 6¼ (6¾, 7¼, 7¾, 8¼, 8½, 8¾)″ (16 [17, 18.5, 19.5, 21, 21.5, 22] cm) from underarm CO, removing markers and ending after a RS row.

Shape Neck

SET-UP ROW: (WS) K59 (64, 71, 78, 84, 90, 96), pm, k17 (19, 21, 23, 25, 27, 29), pm, work to end.

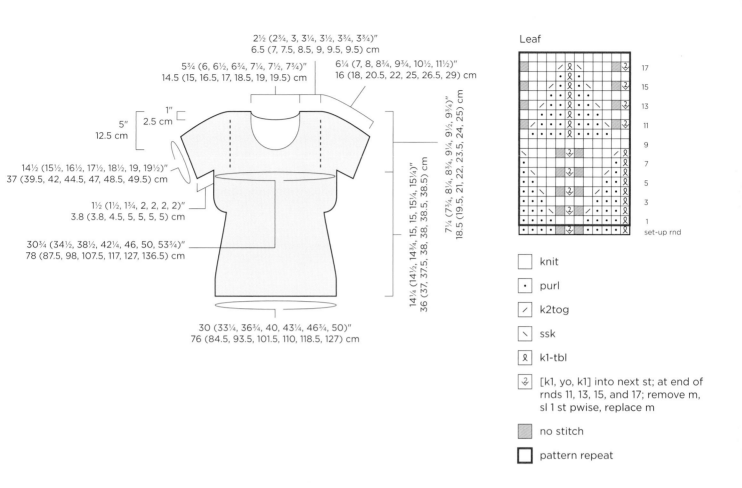

2½ (2¾, 3, 3¼, 3½, 3¾, 3¾)"
6.5 (7, 7.5, 8.5, 9, 9.5, 9.5) cm

5¾ (6, 6½, 6¾, 7¼, 7½, 7¾)"
14.5 (15, 16.5, 17, 18.5, 19, 19.5) cm

6¼ (7, 8, 8¾, 9¾, 10½, 11½)"
16 (18, 20.5, 22, 25, 26.5, 29) cm

1"
2.5 cm

5"
12.5 cm

14½ (15½, 16½, 17½, 18½, 19, 19½)"
37 (39.5, 42, 44.5, 47, 48.5, 49.5) cm

1½ (1½, 1¾, 2, 2, 2, 2)"
3.8 (3.8, 4.5, 5, 5, 5, 5) cm

30¾ (34½, 38½, 42¼, 46, 50, 53¾)"
78 (87.5, 98, 107.5, 117, 127, 136.5) cm

7¼ (7¾, 8¼, 8¾, 9¼, 9½, 9¾)"
18.5 (19.5, 21, 22, 23.5, 24, 25) cm

14¼ (14½, 14¾, 15, 15, 15¼, 15¼)"
36 (37, 37.5, 38, 38, 38.5, 38.5) cm

30 (33¼, 36¾, 40, 43¼, 46¾, 50)"
76 (84.5, 93.5, 101.5, 110, 118.5, 127) cm

Leaf

Chart rows: set-up rnd, 1, 3, 5, 7, 9, 11, 13, 15, 17

☐	knit
•	purl
╱	k2tog
╲	ssk
ℓ	k1-tbl
↯	[k1, yo, k1] into next st; at end of rnds 11, 13, 15, and 17; remove m, sl 1 st pwise, replace m
▨	no stitch
☐	pattern repeat

NEXT ROW: (RS) Purl to first m, join a second ball of yarn and BO 17 (19, 21, 23, 25, 27, 29) marked center sts, work to end—59 (64, 71, 78, 84, 90, 96) sts rem each side.

Work each side separately as foll:

NEXT 4 ROWS: Work to neck edge; on other side, BO 4 sts, work to end—51 (56, 63, 70, 76, 82, 88) sts rem each side after all 4 rows have been worked.

Work 2 rows even.

Place all sts onto holder or waste yarn. Cut yarn and set aside.

casting on and picking up sleeve stitches

The sleeves in this pullover (as well as Whisper on page 58), are worked as a continuation of the upper back and front(s). Whether you're working a pullover or cardigan, you'll begin by using the cable method (see Glossary) to cast on stitches for each sleeve at the base of the armhole, work the upper back and back half of the sleeves to the shoulders, then slip the shoulder sts onto a holder. Stitches for the pullover and cardigan front(s) are worked differently.

Pullover Front: With right side of back facing, hold sleeve CO sts so they are upside down with the RS facing and, beginning at the back left sleeve cuff, pick up and knit the desired number of stitches across the cast-on edge for the left sleeve; with right side of front facing, work across the front stitches, then, with right side of back facing, hold sleeve CO sts so they are upside down with the RS facing and, beginning at the underarm, pick up and knit the desired number of stitches across the cast-on edge for the right sleeve.

Cardigan Front: When working the first right-side row of the left front, with right side of back facing, hold sleeve CO sts so they are upside down with the RS facing and, beginning at the back left sleeve cuff, pick up and knit the desired number of stitches across the cast-on edge for the left sleeve, then work to the end of the left front. When working the first right-side row of the right front, work across the existing stitches of the right front, then, with right side of back facing, hold sleeve CO sts so they are upside down with the RS facing and, beginning at the underarm, pick up and knit the desired number of stitches across the cast-on edge of the right sleeve.

Front

Return 97 (109, 121, 133, 145, 157, 169) held front sts onto longer cir needle. With WS of back facing, twist sleeve CO sts so they are upside down with the RS facing (see box at left). With empty end of cir needle, pick up and knit 9 (9, 10, 11, 11, 12, 12) sts along the CO sts, work in Rev St st to end, then with WS of back facing, twist sleeve CO sts so they are upside down with the RS facing and pick up and knit 9 (9, 10, 11, 11, 12, 12) sts along the CO sts for the other sleeve—115 (127, 141, 155, 167, 181, 193) sts total.

Work 3 rows in Rev St st, ending after a WS row.

Shape Sleeve Caps

Note: Front neck shaping is introduced while sleeve cap shaping is in progress; read all the way through the foll sections before proceeding.

SET-UP ROW: (RS) P26 (30, 35, 39, 43, 48, 52), pm, p63 (67, 71, 77, 81, 85, 89), pm, purl to end.

INC ROW: (WS) Knit to 1 st before m, M1L, k1, sl m, knit to next m, sl m, k1, M1R, knit to end—2 sts inc'd.

Purl 1 RS row.

Rep the last 2 rows 2 (2, 2, 3, 3, 3, 3) more times—121 (133, 147, 163, 175, 189, 201) sts.

[Rep inc row, work 3 rows even in Rev St st] 7 (7, 8, 8, 9, 9, 10) times and *at the same time* when sleeves measure 2¼ (2¾, 3¼, 3¾, 4¼, 4½, 4¾)" (5.5 [7, 8.5, 9.5, 11, 11.5, 12] cm) from underarm CO, ending after a RS row, shape neck as foll.

Shape Neck

SET-UP ROW: (WS) Knit and pm each side of center 7 (9, 11, 13, 15, 17, 19) sts.

NEXT ROW: (RS) Working sleeve cap shaping as required, work to first neck marker, join a second ball of yarn, and BO 7 (9, 11, 13, 15, 17, 19) marked center sts, work to end.

Cont working sleeve cap shaping as required, work each side separately as foll:

NEXT 4 ROWS: Work to neck edge; on other side, BO 3 sts, work to end.

DEC ROW: (WS) Work to 3 sts before neck edge, k2tog, k1; on other side, k1, ssk, work to end—1 st dec'd each side.

Purl 1 RS row.

Rep the last 2 rows 6 more times.

Cont in Rev St st until sleeves measure 7¼ (7¾, 8¼, 8¾, 9¼, 9½, 9¾)" (18.5 [19.5, 21, 22, 23.5, 24, 25] cm) from underarm CO—51 (56, 63, 70, 76, 82, 88) sts rem each side after all shaping is completed.

Join Shoulders

Return 51 (56, 63, 70, 76, 82, 88) held sts from one back shoulder onto needles. Hold needles with front and back sts parallel so that RS face tog and use the three-needle method (see Glossary) to BO sts tog so that seam is on WS of garment. Rep for second shoulder.

Finishing

Block to measurements (see Glossary).

Neck Trim

With shorter cir needle, RS facing, and beg at right shoulder seam, pick up and knit 96 (100, 104, 108, 112, 116, 120) sts evenly spaced (about 3 sts for every 4 rows and 1 st in each BO st) around neck edge.

Pm and join for working in rnds. Work in twisted 1x1 rib for 6 rnds.

BO all sts in patt.

Sleeve Trim

With dpns, RS facing, and beg at underarm, pick up and knit 80 (86, 92, 98, 104, 110, 116) sts evenly spaced (about 3 sts for every 4 rnds) around sleeve edge.

Pm and join for working in rnds. Work in twisted 1x1 rib for 6 rnds.

BO all sts in patt.

Weave in loose ends.

balance PULLOVER

Beginning with a provisional cast-on along the back bodice and sleeves, the yoke and sleeves of this pullover are worked in ribs that run up over the shoulders—with a few increases and decreases to shape the sleeve caps—then down to the lower front bodice. The sleeve stitches are joined with a three-needle bind-off, then the body is worked in rounds in a relatively simple Fair Isle pattern for a fine balance of texture and color.

finished size

About 32 (36, 39¾, 43¾, 47¾, 51½, 55½)" (81.5 [91.5, 101, 111, 121.5, 131, 141] cm) bust circumference.
Sweater shown measures 36" (91.5 cm).

yarn

DK weight (#3 Light).

SHOWN HERE: Amy Butler Belle Organic DK (50% organic wool, 50% organic cotton; 131 yd [119 m]/ 50 g): #05 basil (A), 6 (7, 8, 8, 9, 10, 10) balls; #17 zinc (B), 3 (3, 3, 3, 4, 4, 4) balls; #15 slate (C), 3 (3, 3, 4, 4, 4, 4) balls.

needles

RIBBING: size U.S. 4 (3.5 mm): 16" (40 cm) and two 40" (100 cm) circular (cir).

FAIR ISLE PATT: size U.S. 5 (3.75 mm): 32" (80 cm) cir.
Adjust needle size if necessary to obtain the correct gauge.

notions

Size G/6 (4 mm) crochet hook and waste yarn for provisional CO; markers (m); tapestry needle.

gauge

21 sts and 33 rows = 4" (10 cm) in k2, p2 rib on smaller needles.

24½ sts and 28 rows = 4" (10 cm) in Fair Isle St st on larger needles.

Sleeves and Bodice

With smaller, longer cir needle, waste yarn, and crochet hook, use the crochet chain method (see Glossary) to provisionally CO 280 (296, 312, 320, 328, 344, 352) sts. Do not join. Work back and forth in rows as foll:

With A, knit 1 RS row, then work 2 rows in k2, p2 rib (see Stitch Guide).

SET-UP ROW: (WS) P1, [p2, k2] 27 (29, 30, 31, 31, 33, 33) times, place marker (pm), p2, [k2, p2] 15 (15, 17, 17, 19, 19, 21) times, pm, [k2, p2] 27 (29, 30, 31, 31, 33, 33) times, p1.

Cont for your size as foll:

Sizes 32 (36, 39¾, 43¾, 51½)″ only

INC ROW: (RS) Keeping in patt, work to m, M1 (see Glossary) or M1P (see Glossary) as necessary to maintain patt, slip marker (sl m), work to next m, sl m, M1 or M1P as necessary to maintain patt, work to end—2 sts inc'd.

Work 3 rows even in patt. Working inc'd sts in established ribbing, rep the last 4 rows 2 (3, 1, 2, 1) more time(s), ending with a WS row—286 (304, 316, 326, 348) sts.

Sizes 47¾ (55½)″ only

Skip to all sizes.

All sizes

INC ROW: (RS) Keeping in patt, work to m, M1 or M1P (see Glossary) as necessary to maintain patt, slip marker (sl m), work to next m, sl m, M1 or M1P as necessary to maintain patt, work to end—2 sts inc'd.

Work 1 row even. Rep the last 2 rows 11 (10, 16, 15, 22, 20, 26) times, then work inc row once again—312 (328, 352, 360, 376, 392, 408) sts.

Divide for Neck

With WS facing and keeping in patt, work to first m, sl m, work 10 (10, 14, 14, 18, 18, 22) sts, join a second ball of yarn and BO 42 sts, work to end—135 (143, 155, 159, 167, 175, 183) sts rem each side.

Working each side separately, work in patt for 8 rows, ending with a WS row.

Shape Cap

DEC ROW: (RS) Keeping in patt, work to 2 sts before m, ssk or ssp (see Glossary) as necessary to maintain patt, sl

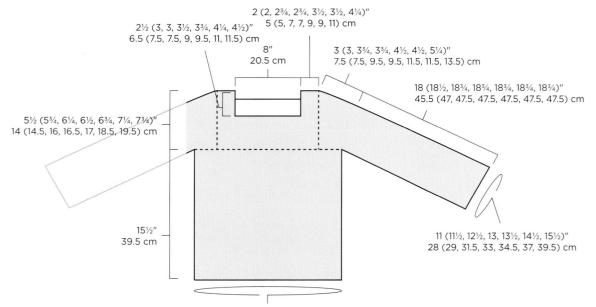

2 (2, 2¾, 2¾, 3½, 3½, 4¼)"
5 (5, 7, 7, 9, 9, 11) cm

2½ (3, 3, 3½, 3¾, 4¼, 4½)"
6.5 (7.5, 7.5, 9, 9.5, 11, 11.5) cm

8"
20.5 cm

3 (3, 3¾, 3¾, 4½, 4½, 5¼)"
7.5 (7.5, 9.5, 9.5, 11.5, 11.5, 13.5) cm

18 (18½, 18¾, 18¾, 18¾, 18¾, 18¾)"
45.5 (47, 47.5, 47.5, 47.5, 47.5, 47.5) cm

5½ (5¾, 6¼, 6½, 6¾, 7¼, 7¾)"
14 (14.5, 16, 16.5, 17, 18.5, 19.5) cm

15½"
39.5 cm

11 (11½, 12½, 13, 13½, 14½, 15½)"
28 (29, 31.5, 33, 34.5, 37, 39.5) cm

32 (36, 39¾, 43¾, 47¾, 51½, 55½)"
81.5 (91.5, 101, 111, 121.5, 131, 141) cm

Orb

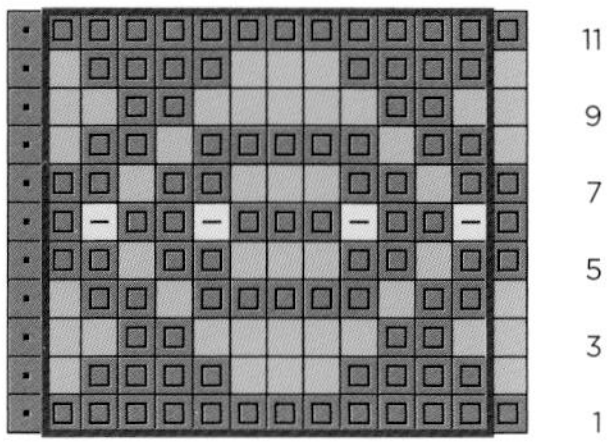

Wave A

Wave B

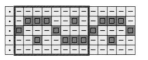

	with A, knit
−	with B, knit
·	with B, purl
▫	with C, knit
▪	with C, purl
▢	pattern repeat

m, work to next m, sl m, k2tog or p2tog as necessary to maintain patt, work to end—1 st dec'd each side.

Work 1 row even. Rep the last 2 rows 9 (11, 11, 13, 14, 16, 18) times—125 (131, 143, 145, 152, 158, 164) sts rem each side.

Cont for your size as foll.

Sizes 32 (39¾, 43¾, 47¾, 51½, 55½)" only

NECK JOINING ROW: (RS) Keeping in patt, work to 2 sts before m, ssk or ssp as necessary to maintain patt, sl m, work to neck edge, turn work so WS is facing, use the cable method (see Glossary) to CO 42 sts, turn work so RS is facing, work to next m, sl m, k2tog or p2tog as necessary to maintain patt, work to end—290 (326, 330, 344, 356, 368) sts rem.

Work 1 row even.

DEC ROW: (RS) Work to 2 sts before m, ssk or ssp as necessary to maintain patt, sl m, work to next m, sl m, k2tog or p2tog as necessary to maintain patt, work to end—2 sts dec'd.

Work 1 row even. Rep the last 2 rows 0 (3, 0, 6, 2, 6) more times—288 (318, 328, 330, 350, 354) sts rem.

Size 36" only

NECK JOINING row: (RS) Keeping in patt, work to neck edge, turn work so WS is facing, use the cable method (see Glossary) to CO 42 sts, turn work so RS is facing, work to end—304 sts.

Work 1 row even.

All sizes

DEC ROW: (RS) Work to 2 sts before m, ssk or ssp as necessary to maintain patt, sl m, work to next m, sl m, k2tog or p2tog as necessary to maintain patt, work to end—2 sts dec'd.

Work 3 rows even. Rep the last 4 rows 3 (3, 2, 3, 0, 2, 0) more times—280 (296, 312, 320, 328, 344, 352) sts rem.

Work 1 RS row even, removing all markers.

Join Sleeves

With WS facing, carefully remove waste yarn from provisional CO and place 280 (296, 312, 320, 328, 344, 352) exposed sts onto a second smaller longer cir needle. On each needle, place a removable marker after first and before last 95 (97, 99, 99, 98, 99, 98) sts for sleeves—90 (102, 114, 122, 132, 146, 156) sts between markers. Hold the needles parallel so that RS of sleeve face tog (so seam will be on WS), then use the three-needle method (see Glossary) to join 95 (97, 99, 99, 98, 99, 98) sleeve sts tog (when binding off the last st, knit the first st from the front to BO rather than knitting 1 from each needle), slip the st rem from the BO onto larger cir needle and knit across front sts to next marker, pm between back and front, slip the next 90 (102, 114, 122, 132, 146, 156) back sts onto the other end of the larger cir needle and set aside, then cont with the smaller needle, use the three-needle method to join rem 95 (97, 99, 99, 98, 99, 98) sleeve sts tog. Fasten off rem st at end of BO—180 (204, 228, 244, 264, 292, 312) body sts rem.

Body

With RS facing and larger cir needle, pm, then join A to beg of back sts in preparation to work in rnds.

Note: *To avoid a hole at the underarm, you may want to pick up and knit 1 or 2 sts at each underarm on the first rnd and decrease them on the next rnd.*

INC RND: *[K12 (12, 15, 11, 10, 13, 12), M1] 1 (1, 1, 1, 3, 1, 1) time(s), [k11 (13, 14, 10, 9, 12, 11), M1] 6 (6, 6, 10, 8, 10, 12) times, [k12 (12, 15, 11, 10, 13, 12), M1] 1 (1, 1, 1, 3, 1, 1) time(s), sl m; rep from * once—196 (220, 244, 268, 292, 316, 340) sts total; 98 (110, 122, 134, 146, 158, 170) sts each for front and back.

SET-UP WAVE PATT: *Work to m according to Rnd 1 of Wave A (B, A, B, A, B, A) chart, sl m; rep from * once.

Work 4 rnds in patt as established.

SET-UP ORB PATT: *Work to m according to Rnd 1 of Orb chart, sl m; rep from * once.

Work 10 rnds in patt as established.

Rep the last 16 rnds 5 more times, then work Rnds 1–5 of Wave A (B, A, B, A, B, A) chart.

NEXT RND: With A and smaller cir needle, knit.

Work 6 rnds in k2, p2 rib. Loosely BO all sts in patt.

Finishing

Weave in loose ends. Block to measurements (see Glossary).

Neck Edging

With smaller shorter cir needle, RS facing, and beg at back right neck, *pick up and knit 44 sts along back neck (1 st for each BO, and 1 additional st at each end), pm, pick up and knit 20 (24, 24, 28, 28, 32, 36) sts evenly spaced along side edge, pm; rep from * once more across front and second side edge—128 (136, 136, 144, 144, 152, 160) sts total.

SET-UP RND: [P2tog, p1, k2, *p2, k2; rep from * to 3 sts before m, p1, ssp, sl m] 4 times—8 sts dec'd.

Work 1 rnd even as established.

DEC RND: *P2tog or k2tog as necessary to maintain patt, work sts as they appear to 2 sts before m, ssp or ssk as necessary to maintain patt; rep from * 3 more times—8 sts dec'd.

Rep the last 2 rnds 2 more times—96 (104, 104, 112, 112, 120, 128) sts rem.

BO all sts in patt.

tranquility 🍃 TUNIC

This super-soft tunic has an interesting construction that begins with the body and sleeves worked separately in an easy-to-memorize cabled feather-and-fan pattern. The sleeves are joined to the body with decreases positioned along the body "armholes," and the back neck is raised by decreases positioned along the back sleeves. The remaining yoke is worked in the round with some raglan shaping before the bind-off at the neck.

finished size

About 27¼ (31¾, 36¼, 40¾, 45¼, 49¾, 54½)" (69 [80.5, 92, 103.5, 115, 126.5, 138.5] cm) bust circumference.
Tunic shown measures 36¼" (92 cm).

yarn

Sportweight (#2 Fine).

SHOWN HERE: The Fibre Company Road to China Light (65% baby alpaca, 15% silk, 10% camel, 10% cashmere; 159 yd [145 m]/50 g): autumn jasper, 6 (8, 9, 10, 11, 12, 14) skeins.

needles

BODY AND SLEEVES: size U.S. 4 (3.5 mm): 32" (60 cm) circular (cir) and set of 4 or 5 double-pointed (dpn).

BACK AND YOKE: size U.S. 1 (2.25 mm): 32" (80 cm) cir.

Adjust needle size if necessary to obtain the correct gauge.

notions

Cable needle (cn); markers (m); stitch holders or waste yarn; tapestry needle.

gauge

30 sts and 28 rnds = 4" (10 cm) in lace patt on larger needles.

28 sts and 42 rnds = 4" (10 cm) in garter st on smaller needles.

Body

With larger cir needle, use the long-tail method (see Glossary) to CO 204 (238, 272, 306, 340, 374, 408) sts. Being careful not to twist sts, join for working garter st (see Glossary) so that the joining bump is on the RS. Place marker (pm) to denote beg of rnd.

Knit 1 rnd. Purl 1 rnd. Knit 1 rnd.

Working the red rep box only, work Rnds 1–8 of Lace chart 16 times, then work Rnds 1–6 again—piece measures about 19½" (49.5 cm) from CO.

INC RND: K1f&b (see Glossary) and replace m between the 2 sts just formed, *[yo, k1] 2 times, yo, [ssk] 3 times, [k2tog] 3 times, [yo, k1] 2 times, yo, k1; rep from * 5 (6, 7, 8, 9, 10, 11) more times, ending last rep before the final k1**, k1f&b and replace m between the 2 sts just formed; rep from * to ** once more—206 (240, 274, 308, 342, 376, 410) sts total; 103 (120, 137, 154, 171, 188, 205) sts each for front and back.

Cut yarn and set aside.

Lace

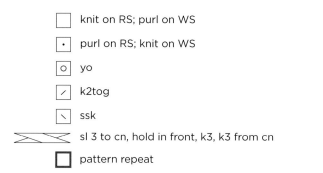

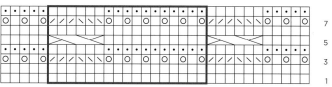

knit on RS; purl on WS

· purl on RS; knit on WS

o yo

╱ k2tog

╲ ssk

sl 3 to cn, hold in front, k3, k3 from cn

pattern repeat

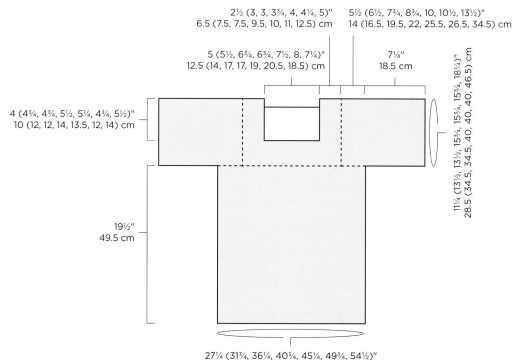

2½ (3, 3, 3¾, 4, 4¼, 5)"
6.5 (7.5, 7.5, 9.5, 10, 11, 12.5) cm

5½ (6½, 7¾, 8¾, 10, 10½, 13½)"
14 (16.5, 19.5, 22, 25.5, 26.5, 34.5) cm

5 (5½, 6¾, 6¾, 7½, 8, 7¼)"
12.5 (14, 17, 17, 19, 20.5, 18.5) cm

7¼"
18.5 cm

4 (4¾, 4¾, 5½, 5¼, 4¾, 5½)"
10 (12, 12, 14, 13.5, 12, 14) cm

11¼ (13½, 13½, 15¾, 15¾, 15¾, 18¼)"
28.5 (34.5, 34.5, 40, 40, 40, 46.5) cm

19½"
49.5 cm

27¼ (31¾, 36¼, 40¾, 45¼, 49¾, 54½)"
69 (80.5, 92, 103.5, 115, 126.5, 138.5) cm

Sleeves

With larger dpn, use the long-tail method to CO 85 (102, 102, 119, 119, 119, 136) sts. Join for working in rnds and pm as before.

Knit 1 rnd. Purl 1 rnd. Knit 1 rnd.

Working red rep box only, work Rnds 1–8 of Lace chart 6 times—piece measures about 7¼″ (18.5 cm) from CO.

Make another sleeve to match.

Join Body and Sleeves

SET-UP ROW: (RS) With RS facing, remove beg-of-rnd marker from body sts, work 85 (102, 102, 119, 119, 119, 136) sleeve sts as foll: k1, replace m, work Row 1 of Lace chart to end of sleeve sts, pm, pick up and knit 1 st from the row below the last body st (to prevent a gap at the underarm) and slip it onto the left needle tip, then knit it tog with the first body st as k2tog, turn work—84 (101, 101, 118, 118, 118, 135) sleeve sts between sleeve markers.

Note: You may find it easiest to turn the corner if you work the first few rows with both the dpn and cir needles.

Cont working sleeve sts back and forth in short-rows while joining the last st of each sleeve to the body as foll:

SHORT-ROW 1: (WS) Sl 1 purlwise with yarn in front (pwise wyf), slip marker (sl m), work as charted to next m, sl m, ssp (last st of sleeve with next body st; see Glossary), turn work—1 body st dec'd.

SHORT-ROW 2: (RS) Sl 1 purlwise with yarn in back (pwise wyb), sl m, work as charted to next m, sl m, k2tog (last st of sleeve with next body st), turn work—1 body st dec'd.

Rep these 2 short-rows 17 (21, 25, 29, 33, 37, 45) more times, then work Short-Row 1 once more to end with WS Row 6 of patt. Move first marker 1 st to the right; move second marker 1 st to the left—84 (97, 110, 123, 136, 149, 158) sts rem each for back and front; 86 (103, 103, 120, 120, 120, 137) sts between markers for sleeve. Cut yarn for first sleeve; keep yarn attached for second sleeve.

working with hand-dyed yarns

It is common for each skein of a hand-dyed yarn to have a slightly different color tone due to variations in the dyeing process. To prevent these subtle but noticeable color shifts every time a new skein is introduced, alternate two skeins throughout the garment. If working in rows, alternate skeins every two rows and carry the unused yarn along the selvedge. If working in rounds, alternate skeins every one or two rounds and carry the unused yarn along the end-of-round "seam." This will obscure the inevitable color variations by spreading them out over a much larger area.

Slip half of the body sts so needle tips are at the side m. Work the second sleeve centered over the side marker in the same manner but do not turn work at the end of the last WS row—65 (74, 83, 92, 101, 110, 111) sts rem each for back and front; 86 (103, 103, 120, 120, 120, 137) sts between markers for each sleeve. Keep markers placed between sleeve and body sts.

Back

The back neck is shaped by working the back neck sts in garter st while dec the sleeve sts at each end of every short-row as foll:

Change to smaller cir needle.

SET-UP ROW: (WS) Sl 1 pwise wyf (last sleeve st), remove m, k1, pm, knit back sts to 1 st before next m, pm, ssp while removing next m, turn work—1 right sleeve st dec'd; markers are now 1 st in from each edge of back—63 (72, 81, 90, 99, 108, 109) sts between markers for back.

SHORT-ROW 1: (RS) Sl 1 pwise wyb, sl m, knit to next m, sl m, k2tog, turn work—1 left sleeve st dec'd.

SHORT-ROW 2: (WS) Sl pwise wyf, sl m, knit to next m, sl m, ssp, turn work—1 right sleeve st dec'd.

Rep these two short-rows 14 (17, 17, 22, 20, 17, 21) more times, then work Short-Row 1 once again but do not turn work at end of last RS row. Move right back marker 1 st to the right and the left back marker 1 st to the left; the left back marker is now the beg of the rnd—270 (316, 334, 376, 398, 422, 450) sts rem; 65 (74, 83, 92, 101, 110, 111) sts each for back and front, 70 (84, 84, 96, 98, 101, 114) sts for each sleeve.

Yoke

With RS facing, join to work in rnds. Purl 1 rnd even.

DEC RND: K2tog, knit to 2 sts before m, ssk, sl m; rep from *—8 sts dec'd.

Rep the last 2 rnds 14 (17, 17, 21, 23, 26, 29) more times—150 (172, 190, 200, 206, 206, 210) sts rem; 35 (38, 47, 48, 53, 56, 51) sts each for front and back, 40 (48, 48, 52, 50, 47, 54) sts for each sleeve.

Loosely BO all sts pwise.

Finishing

Weave in loose ends. Block to measurements (see Glossary), pinning the CO edges to accentuate the scallops.

light ❧ BOLERO

The design for this bolero came about one hot summer day when office air-conditioning blew me chilly. I longed for something to cover my shoulders and protect me from the cold, but I wanted it to be airy enough to wear in the warm outdoors. This lacy cotton shrug fits the bill. Knitted in a single piece that's shaped from the right sleeve, across the back, and ends at the left sleeve, it's a bit more challenging, but well worth the effort.

finished size

About 30½ (35½, 38½, 42½, 46½, 50½, 54½)" (77.5 [90, 98, 108, 118, 128.5, 138.5] cm) bust circumference, fastened.

Bolero shown measures 35½" (90 cm).

yarn

Aran weight (#4 Medium).

SHOWN HERE: Debbie Bliss Eco Aran Fair Trade (100% organic cotton; 82 yd [75 m]/50 g): #622 teal, 8 (8, 9, 9, 10, 10, 11) balls.

needles

SLEEVE RIDGES: size U.S. 8 (5 mm): set of 5 double-pointed (dpn).

SLEEVE AND BODY LACE: size U.S. 9 (5.5 mm): 32" (80 cm) circular (cir) and set of 5 dpn.

TRIM: size U.S. 9 (5.5 mm): 40" (100 cm) cir.

Adjust needle size if necessary to obtain the correct gauge.

notions

Markers (m); stitch holders or waste yarn; one 1" (2.5 cm) button.

gauge

17 sts and 24 rows = 4" (10 cm) in lace patt on larger needles.

18 sts and 27 rows = 4" (10 cm) in ridges patt on smaller needles.

Note: Row gauge is important for the proper fit; see sidebar on page 112.

Right Sleeve

With smaller dpn, use the long-tail method (see Glossary) to CO 49 (49, 55, 55, 55, 61, 61) sts. Being careful not to twist sts, join for working Rev St st (see Glossary). Place marker (pm) for beg of rnd.

Purl 4 rnds. Work 32 rnds in ridges patt (see Stitch Guide). Knit 2 rnds.

Change to larger dpn and beg and end as indicated for your size, work Rnds 1–4 of Lace chart.

INC RND: K1, M1 (see Glossary), work in patt to last st, M1, k1—2 sts inc'd.

Work 7 (3, 7, 5, 3, 5, 3) rnds even in patt. Rep the last 8 (4, 8, 6, 4, 6, 4) rnds 4 (1, 4, 3, 2, 6, 5) more time(s)—59 (53, 65, 63, 61, 75, 73) sts.

Cont for your size as foll.

Sizes 35½ (42½, 46½, 54½)″ only
Rep inc rnd, work 5 (7, 5, 5) rnds even in patt. Rep the last 6 (8, 6, 6) rnds 4 (1, 4, 2) more time(s)—63 (67, 71, 79) sts.

All sizes

Work 4 (6, 4, 4, 2, 2, 2) rnds even, ending with Rnd 12 of chart—59 (63, 65, 67, 71, 75, 79) sts; piece measures about 13¾″ (35 cm) from CO.

Body

Using the cable method (see Glossary), CO 30 (30, 36, 36, 42, 42, 42) sts.

JOINING ROW: (RS) Knit the newly CO sts, work the sleeve sts in patt, then pick up and knit 30 (30, 36, 36, 42, 42,

42) sts along CO edge—119 (123, 137, 139, 155, 159, 163) sts total.

Using 2 cir needles if the sts are too tight to work comfortably on a single needle, work the charted patt back and forth in rows while maintaining 2 sts at each edge in St st (knit on RS; purl on WS).

Work 1 WS row of Lace chart.

NEXT ROW: (RS; dec 1 st on front, inc 1 st on back) K2tog, work in patt to last st, M1, k1.

Work 3 rows even. Rep the last 4 rows 1 (3, 4, 3, 4, 5, 3) more time(s).

Cont for your size as foll.

Size 35½″ only
NEXT ROW: (RS; dec 1 st on front, inc 1 st on back) K2tog, work in patt to last st, M1, k1.

Work 1 WS row even.

Lace

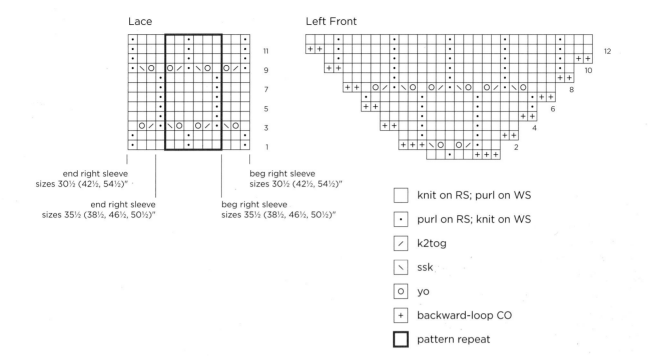

Left Front

end right sleeve
sizes 30½ (42½, 54½)"

beg right sleeve
sizes 30½ (42½, 54½)"

end right sleeve
sizes 35½ (38½, 46½, 50½)"

beg right sleeve
sizes 35½ (38½, 46½, 50½)"

☐	knit on RS; purl on WS
•	purl on RS; knit on WS
╱	k2tog
╲	ssk
○	yo
+	backward-loop CO
▢	pattern repeat

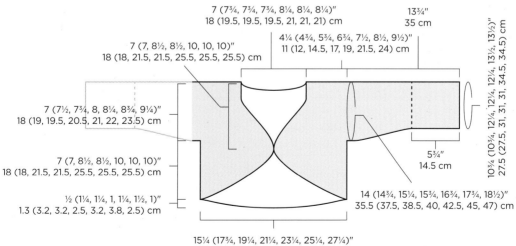

7 (7¾, 7¾, 7¾, 8¼, 8¼, 8¼)"
18 (19.5, 19.5, 19.5, 21, 21, 21) cm

13¾"
35 cm

7 (7, 8½, 8½, 10, 10, 10)"
18 (18, 21.5, 21.5, 25.5, 25.5, 25.5) cm

4¼ (4¾, 5¾, 6¾, 7½, 8½, 9½)"
11 (12, 14.5, 17, 19, 21.5, 24) cm

10¾ (10¾, 12¼, 12¼, 12¼, 13½, 13½)"
27.5 (27.5, 31, 31, 31, 34.5, 34.5) cm

7 (7½, 7¾, 8, 8¼, 8¾, 9¼)"
18 (19, 19.5, 20.5, 21, 22, 23.5) cm

7 (7, 8½, 8½, 10, 10, 10)"
18 (18, 21.5, 21.5, 25.5, 25.5, 25.5) cm

5¾"
14.5 cm

½ (1¼, 1¼, 1, 1¼, 1½, 1)"
1.3 (3.2, 3.2, 2.5, 3.2, 3.8, 2.5) cm

14 (14¾, 15¼, 15¾, 16¾, 17¾, 18½)"
35.5 (37.5, 38.5, 40, 42.5, 45, 47) cm

15¼ (17¾, 19¼, 21¼, 23¼, 25¼, 27¼)"
38.5 (45, 49, 54, 59, 64, 69) cm

DEC ROW: (RS) K2tog, work in patt to end—1 front st dec'd.

Work 1 WS row even. Rep the last 4 rows once more—121 sts rem.

Sizes 30½ (38½, 42½, 46½, 50½, 54½)" only
DEC ROW: (RS) K2tog, work in patt to end—1 front st dec'd.

Work 3 rows even. Rep the last 4 rows 0 (0, 3, 3, 3, 6) more times—118 (136, 135, 151, 155, 156) sts rem.

All sizes
[Rep dec row, then work 1 WS row even] 6 (2, 5, 4, 4, 5, 6) times—112 (119, 131, 131, 147, 150, 150) sts rem; last row worked is Row 2 (6, 12, 6, 10, 4, 10) of chart.

Divide for Neck

With RS facing, k2tog, work until 39 (41, 41, 41, 43, 43, 43) sts are on right needle tip, BO 11 (10, 16, 16, 21, 21, 21) sts, place the first 39 (41, 41, 41, 43, 43, 43) sts onto holder or waste yarn for right front, work to end—61 (67, 73, 73, 82, 85, 85) sts rem for back.

Back

Work 1 WS row even.

DEC ROW: (RS) K2tog, work to end—1 neck st dec'd.

Rep the last 2 rows 3 times—57 (63, 69, 69, 78, 81, 81) sts rem.

Cont even in patt for 27 (31, 31, 31, 35, 35, 35) rows, ending with Row 2 (10, 4, 10, 6, 12, 6) of chart.

INC ROW: (RS) K1, M1, work to end—1 neck st inc'd.

Work 1 WS row even.

Rep the last 2 rows 2 more times, then work inc row once again—61 (67, 73, 73, 82, 85, 85) sts. Place all sts onto holder or waste yarn. Cut yarn and set aside.

Right Front

Return 39 (41, 41, 41, 43, 43, 43) held right front sts to working needle and join yarn in preparation to work a WS row.

Work 1 WS row even.

checking row gauge

For most sweaters worked from the bottom up or the top down, the stitch gauge, which determines the width of the knitting, is more important than the row gauge, which determines the length. For most patterns, you can simply work the number of rows necessary to achieve the desired length. For garments knitted from side to side like this shrug, however, the row gauge becomes more important because it determines the width of the garment. Be sure to work at the proper row gauge to achieve the proper fit.

DEC ROW: (RS) K2tog, work to last 2 sts, ssk—2 sts dec'd.

Rep the last 2 rows 3 (4, 4, 4, 5, 5, 5) more times—31 sts rem.

BO 2 sts at the beg of next 10 rows—11 sts rem.

BO 3 sts at the beg of next 2 rows—5 sts rem.

BO rem sts.

Left Front

CO 5 sts. Begin with a WS row, work Rows 1–13 of Left Front chart—31 sts. Beg with Row 3 (9, 3, 9, 3, 9, 3) of Lace chart, cont in lace patt as established and shape front as foll:

INC ROW: (RS) K1, M1, work to last st, M1, k1—2 sts inc'd.

Work 1 WS row even.

Rep the last 2 rows 2 (3, 3, 3, 4, 4, 4) times, then work inc row again—39 (41, 41, 41, 43, 43, 43) sts; Row 9 (5, 11, 5, 1, 7, 1) of chart has been completed. Cut yarn; leave sts on needle.

Left Body

With WS of back and left front facing, return back sts to the needle with the left front sts so the back sts will be worked first.

JOINING ROW: (WS) Work 61 (67, 73, 73, 82, 85, 85) back sts, use the backward-loop method (see Glossary) to CO 11 (10, 16, 16, 21, 21, 21) sts, work 39 (41, 41, 41, 43, 43, 43) left front sts—111 (118, 130, 130, 146, 149, 149) sts total.

INC ROW: (RS) K1, M1, work in patt to end—1 front st inc'd.

Work 1 WS row even. Rep the last 2 rows 5 (3, 4, 3, 3, 4, 5) more times—117 (122, 135, 134, 150, 154, 155) sts; Row 10 (2, 10, 2, 10, 6, 2) of chart has been completed.

Cont for your size as foll.

Sizes 30½ (38½, 42½, 46½, 50½, 54½)" only
Rep inc row, then work 3 rows even. Rep the last 4 rows 1 (1, 4, 4, 4, 7) more time(s)—119 (137, 139, 155, 159, 163) sts; Row 6 (6, 10, 6, 2, 10) of chart has been completed.

Size 35½" only
NEXT ROW: (RS; inc 1 on front, dec 1 on back) K1, M1, work to last 2 sts, ssk.

Work 1 WS row even, ending with Row 6 of chart.

INC ROW: (RS) K1, M1, work to end—1 front st inc'd.

Work 1 WS row even—123 sts.

All sizes

NEXT ROW: (RS "shift" row; inc 1 on front, dec 1 on back) K1, M1, work to last 2 sts, ssk.

Work 3 rows even. Rep the last 4 rows 0 (3, 3, 2, 3, 4, 2) more times.

Rep "shift" row, then work 1 WS row even—119 (123, 137, 139, 155, 159, 163) sts; Row 12 of chart completed.

Join Body Stitches

Toward the center of the work, pull the circular needle cord through the work and arrange sts so that the ends of the work are at opposite needle tips. With WS facing, use the three-needle method (see Glossary) to BO first and last 30 (30, 36, 36, 42, 42, 42) body sts tog (when binding off the last st, knit the first st from the front needle to BO, rather than knitting 1 from each needle), slip rem st from BO onto front needle and turn work so RS faces out—59 (63, 65, 67, 71, 75, 79) sts rem. Pm for beg of rnd.

Left Sleeve

Change to larger dpn and join for working in rnds. Cont even in patt for 12 (12, 12, 12, 8, 8, 8) rnds, ending with Rnd 12 (12, 12, 12, 8, 8, 8) of chart.

DEC RND: K2tog, work to last 2 sts, ssk—2 sts dec'd.

Work 7 (5, 7, 7, 5, 5, 5) rnds even. Rep the last 8 (6, 7, 7, 6, 6, 6) rnds 3 (3, 3, 0, 3, 5, 1) more time(s)—51 (55, 57, 65, 63, 63, 75) sts rem. Rep dec rnd, then work 3 (3, 3, 5, 3, 3, 3) rnds even. Rep the last 4 (4, 4, 6, 4, 4, 4) rnds 0 (2, 0, 3, 3, 0, 6) more times—49 (49, 55, 57, 55, 61, 61) sts rem.

Cont for your size as foll.

Size 42½" only

Rep dec rnd, then work 3 rnds even—55 sts rem.

All sizes

All sizes end with Rnd 12 of patt.

Change to smaller dpn. Knit 2 rnds, then purl 4 rnds.

Work Rnds 1–8 of ridges patt 4 times.

BO all sts purlwise.

Finishing

Weave in loose ends. Block to measurements (see Glossary).

Edging

With larger cir needle, RS facing, and beg at center of back neck, pick up and knit 273 (291 311, 327, 358, 374, 390) sts (about 3 sts for every 4 rows and 1 st for each st around front opening) evenly spaced around entire edge. Pm and join for working in rnds. Purl 1 rnd, placing an additional m at right front point (last 5 sts BO at end of right front) for buttonhole placement.

BUTTONHOLE ROW: Purl to 2 sts before buttonhole m, p2tog, remove m, [yo] 2 times, p2tog, purl to end.

NEXT ROW: Purl to double yo, p1f&b (see Glossary) into double yo, purl to end.

BO all sts purlwise.

Sew button to left front point, opposite buttonhole.

grace ❧ CARDI

Side-to-side construction makes this cardigan interesting in style and technique. Beginning at the center back, each half of the bodice is worked outward to the sleeve cuff. Stitches for the body are picked up around the lower edge of the bodice and worked downward to the lower edge. The sleeves and lower body are bordered with pearl brioche stitch—one of my favorite patterns for simple texture!

finished size

About 31 (34½, 38, 41½, 44¾, 48¼, 51¾)" (78.5 [87.5, 96.5, 105.5, 113.5, 122.5, 131.5] cm) bust circumference, including about ¾" (2 cm) overlap along buttonband.

Cardigan shown measures 34½" (87.5 cm).

yarn

Worsted weight (#4 Medium).

SHOWN HERE: Quince & Company Lark (100% American wool; 134 yd [123 m]/ 50 g): lichen, 8 (8, 9, 10, 11, 12, 13) skeins.

needles

Size U.S. 7 (4.5 mm): straight, 32" (80 cm) circular (cir) and set of 4 or 5 double-pointed (dpn).

Adjust needle size if necessary to obtain the correct gauge.

notions

Removable markers (m); stitch holder or waste yarn; size G/6 (4 mm) crochet hook and waste yarn for provisional CO; seven ¾" (2 cm) buttons; tapestry needle.

gauge

18½ sts and 27 rows = 4" (10 cm) in St st.

16 sts and 34 rows = 4" (10 cm) in pearl brioche st.

Yf-sl-1-yo: Bring yarn to front of work, slip 1 st purlwise, bring yarn over right-hand needle to the back of work, creating a yo—slipped st and yo count as 1 st.

brk1: Knit the slipped and yo sts from the yf-sl-1-yo tog as a single st.

*Brioche Pearl St Worked in Rnds
(multiple of 2 sts)*
RND 1: *P1, yf-sl-1-yo (see above), rep from *.

RND 2: *K1, brk1 (see above); rep from *.

RND 3: *Yf-sl-1-yo, p1; rep from *.

RND 4: *Brk1, k1; rep from *.

Rep Rnds 1–4 for patt.

*Brioche Pearl St Worked in Rows
(multiple of 2 sts + 1)*
SET-UP ROW: (RS) Knit.

ROW 1: (WS) K1, *yf-sl-1-yo (see above), k1; rep from *.

ROW 2: K1, *brk1 (see above), k1, rep from *.

ROW 3: K2, yf-sl-1-yo, *k1, yf-sl-1-yo, rep from * to last 2 sts, k2.

ROW 4: K2, brk1, *k1, brk1; rep from * to last 2 sts, k2.

Rep Rows 1–4 for patt.

NOTES

→ *Each half of the body begins at the center front edge; after the neck shaping is worked, the stitches are set aside. Then a provisional cast-on is used for half of the back, the back neck is shaped, then the back sts are joined with the front sts. The armhole and sleeve cap are shaped with short-rows, then the sleeve is worked to the cuff edge.*

→ *Stitches for the lower body sts are picked up along the lower edge of the bodice and worked downward to the hem.*

Left Front

With straight needle and using the long-tail method (see Glossary), CO 13 (14, 15, 16, 18, 20, 22) sts.

Purl 1 WS row.

Shape Neck

INC ROW: (RS) Knit to last st, M1 (see Glossary), k1—1 st inc'd.

Work 3 rows even in St st (knit RS rows; purl WS rows).

Rep the last 4 rows once—15 (16, 17, 18, 20, 22, 24) sts.

[Rep inc row, then purl 1 WS row] 4 (4, 5, 6, 6, 7, 8) times—19 (20, 22, 24, 26, 29, 32) sts.

Rep inc row once more—20 (21, 23, 25, 27, 30, 33) sts; piece measures 2¾ (2¾, 3, 3¼, 3¼, 3½, 3¾)" (7 [7, 7.5, 8.5, 8.5, 9, 9.5] cm) from CO.

Cut yarn and place sts onto holder or waste yarn and set aside.

Left Back

With straight needle, crochet hook, and waste yarn, use a provisional method (see Glossary) to CO 23 (24, 26, 28, 31, 34, 37) sts. Beg with a WS row, work in St st until piece measures 2¼ (2¼, 2½, 2½, 2¾, 3, 3¼)" (5.5 [5.5, 6.5, 6.5, 7, 7.5, 8.5] cm) from CO, ending after a WS row.

Shape Neck

INC ROW: (RS) K1, M1, knit to end—1 st inc'd.

Purl 1 WS row.

Rep the last 2 rows 2 more times—26 (27, 29, 31, 34, 37, 40) sts.

Rep inc row once more—27 (28, 30, 32, 35, 38, 41) sts; piece measures 3¼ (3¼, 3½, 3½, 3¾, 4, 4¼)" (8.5 [8.5, 9, 9, 9.5, 10, 11] cm from CO.

Left Bodice

JOINING ROW: (WS) P27 (28, 30, 32, 35, 38, 41) left back sts, place marker (pm), use the backward-loop method (see Glossary) to CO 7 (7, 7, 7, 8, 8, 8) sts, place 20 (21, 23, 25, 27, 30, 33) held left front sts onto empty needle in preparation to work a WS row, then purl these sts—54 (56, 60, 64, 70, 76, 82) sts total.

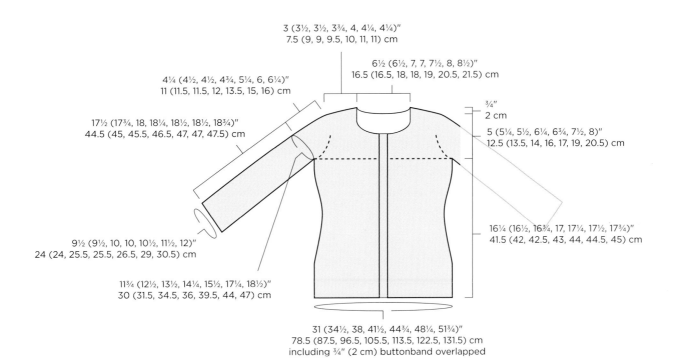

3 (3½, 3½, 3¾, 4, 4¼, 4¼)"
7.5 (9, 9, 9.5, 10, 11, 11) cm

6½ (6½, 7, 7, 7½, 8, 8½)"
16.5 (16.5, 18, 18, 19, 20.5, 21.5) cm

4¼ (4½, 4½, 4¾, 5¼, 6, 6¼)"
11 (11.5, 11.5, 12, 13.5, 15, 16) cm

¾"
2 cm

17½ (17¾, 18, 18¼, 18½, 18½, 18¾)"
44.5 (45, 45.5, 46.5, 47, 47, 47.5) cm

5 (5¼, 5½, 6¼, 6¾, 7½, 8)"
12.5 (13.5, 14, 16, 17, 19, 20.5) cm

16¼ (16½, 16¾, 17, 17¼, 17½, 17¾)"
41.5 (42, 42.5, 43, 44, 44.5, 45) cm

9½ (9½, 10, 10, 10½, 11½, 12)"
24 (24, 25.5, 25.5, 26.5, 29, 30.5) cm

11¾ (12½, 13½, 14¼, 15½, 17¼, 18½)"
30 (31.5, 34.5, 36, 39.5, 44, 47) cm

31 (34½, 38, 41½, 44¾, 48¼, 51¾)"
78.5 (87.5, 96.5, 105.5, 113.5, 122.5, 131.5) cm
including ¾" (2 cm) buttonband overlapped

Work 4 (6, 6, 2, 4, 6, 6) rows even in St st, ending after a WS row.

Shape Shoulder

DEC ROW: (RS) Knit to 3 sts before m, ssk, k1, sl m, k1, k2tog, knit to end—2 sts dec'd.

Work 3 (3, 3, 5, 5, 5, 5) rows even in St st, ending after a WS row.

Rep the last 4 (4, 4, 6, 6, 6, 6) rows 2 times—48 (50, 54, 58, 64, 70, 76) sts rem.

Rep dec row, then work 3 rows even in St st—46 (48, 52, 56, 62, 68, 74) sts rem; piece measures 6½ (6¾, 7, 7¼, 7¾, 8¼, 8½)" (16.5 [17, 18, 18.5, 19.5, 21, 21.5] cm) from provisional CO.

Shape Left Front Armhole

Work short-rows (see Glossary) as foll:

SHORT-ROW 1: With RS facing, k5 (8, 10, 11, 13, 14, 15), wrap next st, turn work so WS is facing, purl to end.

SHORT-ROW 2: With RS facing, k2 (5, 7, 8, 10, 11, 12), wrap next st, turn work so WS is facing, purl to end.

Cont for your size as foll.

Size 31" only

Short-rows are complete.

Sizes 34½ (38, 41½, 44¾, 48¼, 51¾)" only

SHORT-ROW 3: With RS facing, k2 (4, 5, 7, 8, 9), wrap next st, turn work so WS is facing, purl to end.

This completes short-rows for size 34½".

Sizes 38 (41½, 44¾, 48¼, 51¾)" only

SHORT-ROW 4: With RS facing, k3 (4, 6, 7, 8), wrap next st, turn work so WS is facing, purl to end.

SHORT-ROW 5: With RS facing, k2 (3, 5, 6, 7), wrap next st, turn work so WS is facing, purl to end.

This completes short-rows for size 38".

Sizes 41½ (44¾, 48¼, 51¾)" only

SHORT-ROW 6: With RS facing, k2 (4, 5, 6), wrap next st, turn work so WS is facing, purl to end.

This completes short-rows for size 41½".

Sizes 44¾ (48¼, 51¾)" only

SHORT-ROW 7: With RS facing, k3 (4, 5), wrap next st, turn work so WS is facing, purl to end.

SHORT-ROW 8: With RS facing, k2 (3, 4), wrap next st, turn work so WS is facing, purl to end.

This completes short-rows for size 44¾".

Sizes 48¼ (51¾)" only:

SHORT-ROW 9: With RS facing, k2 (3), wrap next st, turn work so WS is facing, purl to end.

This completes short-rows for size 48¼".

Size 51¾" only:

SHORT-ROW 10: (RS) K2, wrap next st, turn work so WS is facing, purl to end.

This completes short-rows for size 51¾".

All sizes

With RS facing, knit to end, hiding wraps with wrapped sts.

Shape Left Back Armhole

Work short-rows as foll:

SHORT-ROW 1: With WS facing, p5 (8, 10, 11, 13, 14, 15), wrap next st, turn work so RS is facing, knit to end.

SHORT-ROW 2: With WS facing, p2 (5, 7, 8, 10, 11, 12), wrap next st, turn work so RS is facing, knit to end.

Cont for your size as foll.

Size 31" only

Short-rows are complete.

Sizes 34½ (38, 41½, 44¾, 48¼, 51¾)" only

SHORT-ROW 3: With WS facing, p2 (4, 5, 7, 8, 9), wrap next st, turn work so RS is facing, knit to end.

This completes short-rows for size 34½".

Sizes 38 (41½, 44¾, 48¼, 51¾)" only

SHORT-ROW 4: With WS facing, p3 (4, 6, 7, 8), wrap next st, turn work so RS is facing, knit to end.

checking gauge in brioche stitch

Because brioche stitch involves yarnovers and slipped stitches, it can be difficult to count the number of stitches and rows when measuring gauge. For the pearl brioche stitch used in Grace, "yf-sl-1-yo" counts as a single stitch, and the pattern appears to repeat over 2 stitches. These slipped stitches also cause the 4-row pattern to appear as if it repeats over 3 rows. The easiest way to count the rows is to count full 4-row repeats, each of which includes one "purl bump." In the illustration below, one pattern repeat of 2 stitches and 4 rows is indicated.

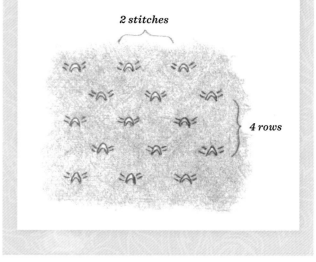

2 stitches

4 rows

SHORT-ROW 5: With WS facing, p2 (3, 5, 6, 7), wrap next st, turn work so RS is facing, knit to end.

This completes short-rows for size 38".

Sizes 41½ (44¾, 48¼, 51¾)" only

SHORT-ROW 6: With WS facing, p2 (4, 5, 6), wrap next st, turn work so RS is facing, knit to end.

This completes short-rows for size 41½".

SHORT-ROW 7: With WS facing, p3 (4, 5), wrap next st, turn work so RS is facing, knit to end.

SHORT-ROW 8: With WS facing, p2 (3, 4), wrap next st, turn work so RS is facing, knit to end.

This completes short-rows for size 44¾″.

Sizes 48¼ (51¾)″ only

SHORT-ROW 9: With WS facing, p2 (3), wrap next st, turn work so RS is facing, knit to end.

This completes short-rows for size 48¼″.

Size 51¾″ only

SHORT-ROW 10: With WS facing, p2, wrap next st, turn work so RS is facing, knit to end.

This completes short-rows for size 51¾″.

All sizes
With WS facing, purl to end, hiding wraps with wrapped sts.

Left Sleeve

Work short-rows as foll:

SHORT-ROW 1: (RS) Knit to m, remove m, k7 (7, 8, 8, 9, 9, 10), wrap next st, turn work.

SHORT-ROW 2: (WS) P14 (14, 16, 16, 18, 18, 20), wrap next st, turn work.

SHORT-ROW 3: (RS) K17 (17, 20, 21, 23, 24, 27), wrap next st, turn work.

SHORT-ROW 4: (WS) P20 (20, 24, 26, 28, 30, 34), wrap next st, turn work.

SHORT-ROW 5: (RS) Knit to wrapped st, work wrap tog with wrapped st to hide wrap, wrap next st, turn work.

SHORT-ROW 6: (WS) Purl to wrapped st, work wrap tog with wrapped st to hide wrap, wrap next st, turn work.

Rep the last 2 short-rows 11 (12, 12, 13, 15, 17, 18) more times.

JOINING RND: (RS) With cir needle or dpn, knit to end of row hiding the wraps when you come to them, then use the backward-loop method to CO 4 (5, 5, 5, 5, 6, 6) sts, pm to denote beg of rnd, then CO 4 (5, 5, 5, 5, 6, 6) sts as before—54 (58, 62, 66, 72, 80, 86) sts total.

Hiding the wrap on the first st of the first rnd, work 6 rnds in St st, working the magic-loop technique (see Glossary) or changing to dpn when there are too few sts to fit comfortably on cir needle.

DEC RND: K1, k2tog, knit to last 3 sts, ssk, k1—2 sts dec'd.

Knit 15 (11, 9, 7, 7, 5, 5) rnds.

Rep the last 16 (12, 10, 8, 8, 6, 6) rnds 2 (5, 4, 5, 9, 6, 13) more times—48 (46, 52, 54, 52, 66, 58) sts rem.

[Rep dec rnd, then knit 17 (13, 11, 9, 9, 7, 7) rnds] 2 (1, 3, 4, 1, 6, 1) time(s)—44 (44, 46, 46, 50, 54, 56) sts rem.

Rep dec rnd once more—42 (42, 44, 44, 48, 52, 54) sts rem.

Cont even in St st until piece measures 14 (14¼, 14½, 14¾, 15, 15, 15¼)″ (35.5 [36, 37, 37.5, 38, 38, 38.5] cm) from joining rnd.

NEXT RND: P5 (5, 6, 6, 3, 5, 3), p2tog, *p8 (8, 8, 8, 6, 6, 7), p2tog; rep from * to last 5 (5, 6, 6, 3, 5, 4) sts, purl to end—38 (38, 40, 40, 42, 46, 48) sts rem.

Work Rnds 1–4 of pearl brioche st worked in rnds (see Stitch Guide) for 3½″ (9 cm), ending after Rnd 1 or 3 of patt.

Loosely BO all sts in patt.

Right Back

Carefully remove waste yarn from provisional CO and place 23 (24, 26, 28, 31, 34, 37) exposed sts onto straight needle and join yarn in preparation to work a WS row. Work even in St st until piece measures 2¼ (2¼, 2½, 2½, 2¾, 3, 3¼)″ (5.5 [5.5, 6.5, 6.5, 7, 7.5, 8.5] cm) from CO, ending after a WS row.

Shape Neck

INC ROW: (RS) Knit to last st, M1, k1—1 st inc'd.

Purl 1 WS row.

Rep the last 2 rows 2 more times—26 (27, 29, 31, 34, 37, 40) sts.

Rep inc row once more—27 (28, 30, 32, 35, 38, 41) sts; piece measures 3¼ (3¼, 3½, 3½, 3¾, 4, 4¼)″ (8.5 [8.5, 9, 9, 9.5, 10, 11] cm) from provisional CO.

Place sts onto holder or waste yarn. Cut yarn and set aside.

Right Front

Using the long-tail method, CO 13 (14, 15, 16, 18, 20, 22) sts.

Purl 1 WS row.

Shape Neck

INC ROW: (RS) K1, M1, knit to end—1 st inc'd.

Work 3 rows even in St st.

Rep the last 4 rows once—15 (16, 17, 18, 20, 22, 24) sts.

[Rep inc row, then purl 1 WS row] 4 (4, 5, 6, 6, 7, 8) times—19 (20, 22, 24, 26, 29, 32) sts.

Rep inc row once more—20 (21, 23, 25, 27, 30, 33) sts; piece measures 2¾ (2¾, 3, 3¼, 3¼, 3½, 3¾)" (7 [7, 7.5, 8.5, 8.5, 9, 9.5] cm) from CO.

Right Bodice

JOINING ROW: (WS) Purl to end of right front sts, use the backward-loop method to CO 7 (7, 7, 8, 8, 8, 8) sts, pm, place 27 (28, 30, 32, 35, 38, 41) held right back sts onto empty needle in preparation to work a WS row, then purl these sts—54 (56, 60, 64, 70, 76, 82) sts total.

Work 4 (6, 6, 2, 4, 6, 6) rows even in St st, ending after a WS row.

Shape Shoulder

Work same as left bodice shoulder.

Shape Right Back Armhole

Work same as left front armhole.

Shape Right Front Armhole

Work same as left back armhole.

Right Sleeve

Work same as left sleeve.

Body

With RS facing, use circular needle to pick up and knit 30 (33, 37, 41, 45, 48, 53) sts evenly spaced along left front to underarm CO sts, 4 (5, 5, 5, 5, 6, 6) underarm sts, pm, 4 (5, 5, 5, 5, 6, 6) underarm sts, 64 (70, 78, 86, 94, 100, 106) sts evenly along back to underarm CO, 4 (5, 5, 5, 5, 6, 6) underarm sts, pm, 4 (5, 5, 5, 5, 6, 6) underarm sts, 30 (33, 37, 41, 45, 48, 53) sts evenly along right front—140 (156, 172, 188, 204, 220, 236) sts total.

Do not join. Purl 1 WS row.

Shape Waist

DEC ROW: (RS) *Knit to 3 sts before m, ssk, k1, sl m, k1, k2tog; rep from * once, knit to end—4 sts dec'd.

Work 3 (5, 5, 5, 5, 7, 7) rows even in St st, ending after a WS row.

Rep the last 4 (6, 6, 6, 6, 8, 8) rows 4 (1, 2, 3, 4, 1, 2) time(s)—120 (148, 160, 172, 184, 212, 224) sts.

Cont for your size as foll.

Sizes 31 (44¾)" only

These sizes are complete.

Sizes 34½ (38, 41½, 48¼, 51¾)" only

[Rep dec row, then work 3 (3, 3, 5, 5) row(s) even] 3 (2, 1, 3, 2) time(s)—136 (152, 168, 200, 216) sts rem.

All sizes

Cont in St st until piece measures 5¾ (6, 6¼, 6½, 6¾, 7, 7¼)" (14.5 [15, 16, 16.5, 17, 18, 18.5] cm) from pick-up row, ending after a WS row.

INC ROW: (RS) Knit to 1 st before m, M1, k1, sl m, k1, M1; rep from * once, knit to end—4 sts inc'd.

Work 9 rows even in St st, ending after a WS row.

Rep the last 10 rows 3 times—136 (152, 168, 184, 200, 216, 232) sts.

Rep inc row once more—140 (156, 172, 188, 204, 220, 236) sts.

Cont in St st until piece measures 12¾ (13, 13¼, 13½, 13¾, 14, 14¼)" (32.5 [33, 33.5, 34.5, 35, 35.5, 36] cm) from pick-up row, ending after a RS row.

DEC ROW: (WS) K6 (5, 4, 3, 18, 1, 0), k2tog, *k7, k2tog; rep from * to last 6 (5, 4, 3, 18, 1, 0) st(s), knit to end—125 (139, 153, 167, 181, 195, 209) sts rem.

Work pearl brioche st in rows (see Stitch Guide) for 3½" (9 cm), ending after Row 1 or 3 of patt.

Loosely BO all sts in patt.

Finishing

Buttonband

With straight needle, RS facing, and beg at left front neck edge, pick up and knit 86 (88, 90, 92, 95, 99, 102) sts evenly spaced (1 st in each CO st and about 3 sts for every 4 rows of St st and 3 sts for every 8 rows of pearl brioche st) along left front edge. Knit 3 rows, ending after a WS row.

Leave sts on needle, cut yarn, and set aside.

Use removable markers to mark placement of 7 buttonholes along right edge, with the first ¾" (2 cm) down from neck edge, the last ¾" (2 cm) up from the lower edge, and the rem 5 evenly spaced in between.

Buttonhole Band

With cir needle, RS facing, and beg at lower right front edge, pick up and knit 86 (88, 90, 92, 95, 99, 102) sts evenly spaced (about 3 sts for every 8 rows of pearl brioche st, 3 sts in every 4 rows in St st along right front edge to bodice, and 1 st for each CO st) along left front edge. Knit 1 WS row.

BUTTONHOLE ROW: (RS) *Knit to buttonhole m, yo, k2tog; rep from * 6 times, knit to end.

Knit 2 rows, ending after a RS row.

Leave sts on needle.

Neckband

With RS facing, rotate work 90° clockwise and pick up and knit 68 (68, 72, 72, 78, 82, 86) sts evenly spaced (about 3 sts for every 4 rows and 1 st in each CO st) along top of bands and neck edge, knit across buttonband sts.

With WS facing, BO all sts kwise.

Weave in loose ends. Block to measurements (see Glossary). Sew buttons opposite buttonholes.

warmth  TOP

Fast and fun, this top can be knitted in a matter of days and leave you longing to start another. It begins at the lower edge with a generous pouch pocket and includes waist shaping for a fitted look. At the armholes, stitches are cast on for the sleeves, then a handful of decrease rounds shape the yoke, and short-rows shape the sleeves. Shown here with a short ribbed collar, this could be made even more inviting with an oversized cowl.

finished size

About 31½ (34½, 37½, 40½, 43¾, 46¾, 49¾)" [80 (87.5, 95, 103, 111, 118.5, 126.5) cm] bust circumference.
Top shown measures 34½" (87.5 cm).

yarn

Bulky (#6 Super Bulky).

SHOWN HERE: Tahki Montana (100% pure wool; 130 yd [119 m]/100 g): #02 bark, 4 (4, 5, 5, 5, 6, 6) skeins.

needles

Size U.S. 13 (9 mm): 24" (60 cm) circular (cir) and set of 4 or 5 double-pointed (dpn).

Adjust needle size if necessary to obtain the correct gauge.

notions

Cable needle (cn); stitch holder; markers (m); tapestry needle.

gauge

10½ sts and 16 rnds = 4" (10 cm) in St st, worked in rnds.

10 sts = 3¼" (8.5 cm) in cable panel, worked in rnds.

Body

With cir needle, use the long-tail method (see Glossary) to CO 84 (92, 100, 108, 116, 124, 132) sts. Place marker (pm) and join for working in rnds, being careful not to twist sts.

SET-UP RIB: P2 (0, 2, 0, 2, 0, 2), *k2, p2; rep from * to last 2 (0, 2, 0, 2, 0, 2) sts, k2 (0, 2, 0, 2, 0, 2).

Work in rib as established for 2 more rnds.

Pocket

Note: When establishing the pocket, the sts for the pocket are doubled by working 2 sts into each st (on page 128). On the following row, the inc'd sts are placed onto a holder to be worked later with the body sts. When slipping the sts onto the holder, move the yarn to the back (RS) and hold the holder in the front of the work (WS). The pocket sts are worked back and forth in rows, then placed onto a holder to be joined with the body later.

NEXT RND: K2 (4, 6, 8, 6, 8, 10) sts, pm, [k1f&b (see Glossary)] 2 times, [p1f&b (see Glossary)] 2 times, [k1f&b] 10 (10, 10, 10, 14, 14, 14) times, [p1f&b] 6 times, [k1f&b] 2 times, [p1f&b] 2 times, [k1f&b] 10 (10, 10, 10, 14, 14, 14) times, [p1f&b] 2 times, k1f&b, k1, pm, turn work—44 (50, 56, 62, 64, 70, 76) sts left unworked.

Cont working back and forth between markers for pocket as foll:

ROW 1: (WS) Sl 1 purlwise with yarn in front (pwise wyf), sl 1 to holder, p1, sl 1 to holder, [k1, sl 1 to holder] 2 times, [p1, sl 1 to holder] 10 (10, 10, 10, 14, 14, 14) times, [k1, sl 1 to holder] 2 times, [p1, sl 1 to holder] 2 times, [k1, sl 1 to holder] 6 times, [p1, sl 1 to holder] 10 (10, 10, 10, 14, 14, 14) times, [k1, sl 1 to holder] 2 times, p1, sl 1 to holder, p1, turn work—38 (38, 38, 38, 46, 46, 46) pocket sts; 37 (37, 37, 37, 45, 45, 45) body sts on holder.

ROW 2: (RS) Sl 1 st pwise with yarn in back (wyb), k1, p2, k10 (10, 10, 10, 14, 14, 14), work 10 sts according to Row 1 of Cable Panel chart, k10 (10, 10, 10, 14, 14, 14), p2, k2.

ROW 3: Sl 1 pwise wyf, p1, k2, p10 (10, 10, 10, 14, 14, 14), work 10 sts according to Row 2 of chart, p10 (10, 10, 10, 14, 14, 14), k2, p2.

DEC ROW: Sl 1 st pwise wyb, k1, p2, k2tog, work in patt as established to last 6 sts, ssk, k2, p2—2 sts dec'd.

Keeping in patt, work 3 rows even. Rep the last 4 rows 4 more times—28 (28, 28, 28, 36, 36, 36) sts rem. Rep dec row once more—26 (26, 26, 26, 34, 34, 34) sts rem.

Work 2 more rows even in patt, ending after RS Row 1 of chart. Place all pocket sts onto holder. Cut yarn.

JOINING RND: (RS) Place 37 (37, 37, 37, 45, 45, 45) held body sts onto left needle tip. Remove pocket marker. Join yarn at right-hand edge of pocket and work as foll: M1 (see Glossary), k17 (17, 17, 17, 21, 21, 21), k2tog, k18 (18, 18, 18, 22, 22, 22), remove pocket marker, M1, k2 (4, 6, 8, 6, 8, 10), pm for side "seam," knit to end of rnd—84 (92, 100, 108, 116, 124, 132) sts total.

Knit 2 rnds.

Shape Waist

DEC RND: *K1, k2tog, knit to next m, ssk, k1; rep from *—4 sts dec'd.

Work 9 rnds even. Rep the last 10 rnds once more—76 (84, 92, 100, 108, 116, 124) sts rem. Rep dec rnd—72 (80, 88, 96, 104, 112, 120) sts rem. Work 3 rnds even.

POCKET JOINING RND: K5 (7, 9, 11, 9, 11, 13), place 26 (26, 26, 26, 34, 34, 34) held pocket sts onto empty needle, join pocket sts by working k2tog or p2tog (1 st each from each needle) as necessary to maintain patt to end of pocket sts, work to end—still 72 (80, 88, 96, 104, 112, 120) sts.

Work 8 (7, 6, 5, 4, 3, 2) rnds even in patt as established.

Shape Bust

INC RND: *K1, M1, work in patt to 1 st before next m, M1, k1; rep from *—4 sts inc'd.

Work 9 rnds even. Rep the last 10 rnds 2 more times—84 (92, 100, 108, 116, 124, 132) sts. Work 1 rnd even, ending after Rnd 17 (16, 15, 14, 13, 12, 11) of chart and ending 3 (3, 3, 3, 4, 4, 4) sts before beg-of-rnd m on last rnd.

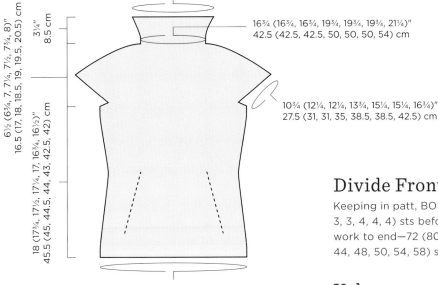

25¼ (25¼, 25¼, 29¾, 29¾, 29¾, 32)"
64 (64, 64, 75.5, 75.5, 75.5, 81.5) cm

3¼"
8.5 cm

16¾ (16¾, 16¾, 19¾, 19¾, 19¾, 21¼)"
42.5 (42.5, 42.5, 50, 50, 50, 54) cm

6½ (6¾, 7, 7¼, 7½, 7¾, 8)"
16.5 (17, 18, 18.5, 19, 19.5, 20.5) cm

10¾ (12¼, 12¼, 13¾, 15¼, 15¼, 16¾)"
27.5 (31, 31, 35, 38.5, 38.5, 42.5) cm

18 (17¾, 17½, 17¼, 17, 16¾, 16½)"
45.5 (45, 44.5, 44, 43, 42.5, 42) cm

31½ (34½, 37½, 40½, 43¾, 46¾, 49¾)"
80 (87.5, 95, 103, 111, 118.5, 126.5) cm

Cable Panel

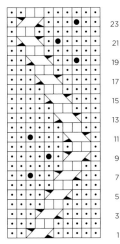

☐ knit

• purl

⬤ MB (see Stitch Guide)

sl 1 st to cn, hold in back, k2, p1 from cn

sl 2 sts to cn, hold in front, p1, k2 from cn

Divide Front and Back

Keeping in patt, BO 6 (6, 6, 6, 8, 8, 8) sts, work to 3 (3, 3, 3, 4, 4, 4) sts before next m, BO 6 (6, 6, 6, 8, 8, 8) sts, work to end—72 (80, 88, 96, 100, 108, 116) sts rem; 36 (40, 44, 48, 50, 54, 58) sts each for front and back.

Yoke

SET-UP ROW: With WS is facing, use the cable method (see Glossary) to CO 22 (26, 26, 30, 32, 32, 36) sts and pm on each side of these CO sts (the first marker placed marks the new beg of rnd), then with RS facing work front sts as established, then turn work so WS is facing and use the cable method to CO 22 (26, 26, 30, 32, 32, 36) sts and pm on each side of these CO sts, then, with RS facing, work back sts as established—116 (132, 140, 156, 164, 172, 188) sts total.

Join for working in rnds and work 3 rnds, working CO sts in St st and ending after Rnd 22 (21, 20, 19, 18, 17, 16) of chart.

Work short-rows (see Glossary) as foll:

With RS facing and keeping in patt, knit to 1 st before first m, wrap next st, turn work so WS is facing, purl to 1 st before beg-of-rnd m, wrap next st, turn work so RS is facing, work to 1 st before last m, wrap next st, turn work so WS is facing, purl to 1 st before next, wrap next st, turn work so RS is facing, knit to end.

Keeping in patt, work 9 (9, 10, 10, 10, 11, 11) rnds even, working the wraps tog with their wrapped sts when you come to them, working CO sts in St st, and ending after Rnd 8 (7, 7, 6, 5, 5, 4) of chart.

knitting a seamless pocket

It's surprisingly easy to work a pocket seamlessly into a single rib pattern. To set up for the pocket, simply double the number of stitches at the base of the pocket by working k1f&b or p1f&b while maintaining the established k1, p1 rib pattern across all but the last pocket stitch (which is worked without increasing) on a right-side row (**Figure 1**). On the following row, divide the increased stitches so that one stitch is kept on the needle to work for the pocket lining and the other stitch is placed on a holder to work later for the body as follows: With wrong side facing, slip the first stitch purlwise with the yarn in the front, *bring yarn to back and slip 1 stitch onto holder, bring yarn to front and work the next stitch as it appears (knit or purl); repeat from * to the last pocket stitch, work the last stitch as it appears—there will be one more stitch on the needle for the pocket lining than will be on the holder for the body

(**Figure 2**). Work the stitches back and forth in rows until the lining is the desired length, decreasing to shape the sides of the pocket if desired, then place these stitches on a separate holder. With right side facing, return the initial held body stitches to the left needle, join the yarn at the right pocket edge and compensate for the 1-stitch difference as follows: Work a M1 increase (see Glossary), work across half of the held stitches, work a k2tog decrease, work to end of the held stitches, the work another M1 increase—2 stitches increased and 1 stitch decreased. Continue working the body until it is the same length as the pocket lining.

To join the top of the pocket, return the held upper pocket sts to a spare needle, hold the 2 needles parallel and *work 1 stitch from each needle together as k2tog; repeat from * until all held stitches have been joined.

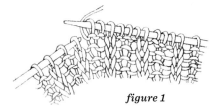

figure 1

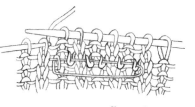

figure 2

Shape Yoke

DEC RND 1: Keeping in patt, work for your size as foll.

Size 31½″ only
K2, [k2tog, k1] 3 times, [k1, ssk] 3 times, [k2, ssk] 2 times, k1, p2, k2tog, k2, work 10 sts as charted, k2, ssk, p2, k1, [k2tog, k2] 2 times, [k2tog, k1] 3 times, [k1, ssk] 3 times, k4, [ssk, k4] 3 times, [k2tog, k4] 2 times, k2tog, k2—92 sts rem.

Size 34½″ only
K1, [k2tog, k1] 4 times, [k1, ssk] 7 times, k1, p2, k2tog, k2, work 10 sts as charted, k2, ssk, p2, k1, [k2tog, k1] 7 times, [k1, ssk] 4 times, [k3, ssk] 4 times, k2, [k2tog, k3] 3 times, k2tog, k2—100 sts rem.

Size 37½″ only
K1, [k2tog, k1] 4 times, [k1, ssk] 8 times, p2, k2tog, k2, work 10 sts as charted, k2, ssk, p2, [k2tog, k1] 8 times, [k1, ssk] 6 times, [k3, ssk] 3 times, k1, [k3, k2tog] 4 times, k1, k2tog—104 sts rem.

Size 40½″ only
[K2tog, k1] 5 times, [k1, ssk] 9 times, k1, p2, k2tog, k2, work 10 sts as charted, k2, ssk, p2, k1, [k2tog, k1] 9 times, [k1, ssk] 5 times, [ssk, k3] 5 times, k1, [k2tog, k3] 4 times, k2tog—116 sts rem.

Sizes 43¾ (46¾)" only

K1, [k2tog, k1] 5 times, [k1, ssk] 7 (5) times, [k2, ssk] 2 (4) times, k1, p2, k2tog, k2, work 10 sts as charted, k2, ssk, p2, k1, [k2tog, k2] 2 (4) times, [k2tog, k1] 7 (5) times, [k1, ssk] 5 times, k2 (4), [ssk, k3] 5 times, k1, [k2tog, k3] 4 times, k2tog, k1 (3)—124 (132) sts rem.

Size 49¾" only

[K2tog, k1] 6 times, [k1, ssk] 9 times, [k2, ssk] 2 times, k1, p2, k2tog, k2, work 10 sts as charted, k2, ssk, p2, k1, [k2tog, k2] 2 times, [k2tog, k1] 9 times, [k1, ssk] 6 times, [ssk, k3] 6 times, k1, [k2tog, k3] 5 times, k2tog—140 sts rem.

All sizes

Rep sleeve short-rows as before.

Keeping in patt, work 3 (3, 3, 4, 4, 4, 5) rnds even, ending after Rnd 13 (12, 12, 12, 11, 11, 11) of chart. From this point on, discontinue bobbles and work those sts as purl sts; cont working cables.

DEC RND 2: Keeping in patt, work for your size as foll.

Size 31½" only

K1, [k2tog] 3 times, k2, [ssk] 3 times, [k1, ssk] 2 times, p2, k2tog, k1, work 10 sts as charted, k1, ssk, p2, [k2tog, k1] 2 times, [k2tog] 3 times, k2, [ssk] 3 times, [k3, ssk] 3 times, k2, [k2tog, k3] 2 times, k2tog, k2—68 sts rem.

Size 34½" only

[K2tog] 4 times, k2, [ssk] 7 times, p2, k2tog, k1, work 10 sts as charted, k1, ssk, p2, [k2tog] 7 times, k2, [ssk] 4 times, [k2, ssk] 4 times, [k2tog, k2] 4 times—68 sts rem.

Size 37½" only

[K2tog] 4 times, k2, [ssk] 7 times, k1, p2, k2tog, k1, work 10 sts as charted, k1, ssk, p2, k1, [k2tog] 7 times, k2, [ssk] 4 times, [k2, ssk] 4 times, k2, [k2tog, k2] 4 times—72 sts rem.

Size 40½" only

K1, [k2tog] 4 times, k2, [ssk] 4 times, k2, [ssk] 4 times, p2, k2tog, k1, work 10 sts as charted, k1, ssk, p2, [k2tog] 4 times, k2, [k2tog] 4 times, k2, [ssk] 4 times, k1, ssk, [k2, ssk] 4 times, [k2, k2tog] 5 times—80 sts rem.

Sizes 43¾ (46¾)" only

[K2tog] 5 times, k2, [ssk] 7 (5) times, [k1, ssk] 2 (4) times, p2, k2tog, k1, work 10 sts as charted, k1, ssk, p2, [k2tog, k1] 2 (4) times, [k2tog] 7 (5) times, k2, [ssk] 5 times, k1

(3), [ssk, k2] 4 times, ssk, [k2, k2tog] 5 times, k1 (3)—84 (92) sts rem.

Size 49¾" only

K1, [k2tog] 5 times, k2, [ssk] 5 times, k2, [ssk] 3 times, [k1, ssk] 2 times, p2, k2tog, k1, work 10 sts as charted, k1, ssk, p2, [k2tog, k1] 2 times, [k2tog] 3 times, k2, [k2tog] 5 times, k2, [ssk] 5 times, k1, ssk, [k2, ssk] 5 times, [k2, k2tog] 6 times—96 sts rem.

All sizes

Keeping in patt, work 4 (4, 4, 5, 5, 5, 5) rnds even, ending after Rnd 18 (17, 17, 18, 17, 17, 17) of chart.

DEC RND 3: Keeping in patt, work for your size as foll.

Size 31½" only

[K2tog] 2 times, k2, [ssk] 3 times, k1, p2tog, k2tog, work 10 sts as charted, ssk, p2tog, k1, [k2tog] 3 times, k2, [ssk] 2 times, [k2, ssk] 3 times, [k2tog, k2] 3 times—48 sts rem.

Size 34½" only

[K2tog] 2 times, k2, [ssk] 3 times, k1, p2tog, k2tog, work 10 sts as charted, ssk, p2tog, k1, [k2tog] 3 times, k2, [ssk] 2 times, k2, [ssk, k1] 3 times, k2, [k1, k2tog] 3 times, k2—48 sts rem.

Size 37½" only

[K2tog] 2 times, k2, [ssk] 4 times, p2tog, k2tog, work 10 sts as charted, ssk, p2tog, [k2tog] 4 times, k2, [ssk] 2 times, k1, [k1, ssk] 4 times, [k2tog, k1] 4 times, k1—48 sts rem.

Size 40½" only

K1, [k2tog] 2 times, k2, [ssk] 2 times, k2, [ssk] 2 times, p2tog, k2tog, work 10 sts as charted, ssk, p2tog, [k2tog] 2 times, k2, [k2tog] 2 times, k2, [ssk] 2 times, k3, [k1, ssk] 4 times, [k2tog, k1] 4 times, k2—56 sts rem.

Sizes 43¾" only

K1, [k2tog] 2 times, k2, ssk, [ssk, k1] 3 times, p2tog, k2tog, work 10 sts as charted, ssk, p2tog, [k1, k2tog] 3 times, k2tog, k2, [ssk] 2 times, k4, [k1, ssk] 4 times, [k2tog, k1] 4 times, k3—60 sts rem.

Sizes 46¾" only

[K2tog] 3 times, [ssk] 7 times, p2tog, k2tog, work 10 sts as charted, ssk, p2tog, [k2tog] 7 times, [ssk] 4 times, [k1, ssk] 5 times, [k2tog, k1] 5 times, k2tog—56 sts rem.

Size 49¾" only

[K2tog] 3 times, k2, [ssk] 7 times, p2tog, k2tog, work 10 sts as charted, ssk, p2tog, [k2tog] 7 times, k2, [ssk] 4 times, [k1, ssk] 5 times, [k2tog, k1] 5 times, k2tog—60 sts rem.

All sizes

Keeping in patt, work 1 (2, 2, 1, 2, 2, 2) rnd(s) even, ending after Rnd 20 of chart.

Discontinue cable panel and work those 10 sts as they appear (knit the knits and purl the purls).

DEC RND 4: K8 (8, 8, 11, 12, 10, 12), p3tog, p5, k2, p1, p3tog, knit to last st, wrap next st, turn work so WS is facing, p16 (16, 16, 18, 20, 20, 20), wrap next st, turn work so RS is facing, knit to end—44 (44, 44, 52, 56, 52, 56) sts rem.

Work 1 rnd even.

Collar

SET-UP RND: *P2, k2; rep from *.

Work 4 more rnds in rib as established.

INC RND: *P1, M1P (see Glossary), p1, k1, M1, k1; rep from *—66 (66, 66, 78, 84, 78, 84) sts.

Work 7 rnds in p3, k3 rib as established.

Loosely BO all sts in patt.

Finishing

Armhole Trim

With RS facing and beg at center of underarm BO, pick up and knit 4 (4, 4, 4, 5, 5, 5) sts along BO edge, 24 (28, 28, 32, 34, 34, 38) sts along sleeve CO sts, then 4 (4, 4, 4, 5, 5, 5) sts along BO edge to end at center of underarm—32 (36, 36, 40, 44, 44, 48) sts total. Pm for beg of rnd.

Dec rnd: Work for your size as foll.

Sizes 31½ (34½, 37½, 40½)" only

K1, p1, p2tog, k2tog, *k1, p2, k1; rep from * to last 6 sts, ssk, p2tog, p1, k1—28 (32, 32, 36) sts rem.

Sizes 43¾ (46¾, 49¾)" only

K1, p2, ssk, k2tog, p2, *k2, p2; rep from * to last 7 sts, ssk, k2tog, p2, k1—40 (40, 44) sts rem.

All sizes

Work 2 rnds in rib as established.

Loosely BO all sts in patt.

Weave in loose ends. Block to measurements (see Glossary).

trust PULLOVER

Worked primarily in stockinette stitch, this casual pullover features a wide ribbed shawl collar and a shaped pouch pocket. The body and sleeves are worked separately to the armholes, at which point the upper body is worked in one piece to the neck, with set-in-sleeve shaping along the way. The simple design and no-fuss finishing make this a trustworthy addition to any wardrobe.

finished size

About 34 (38, 42¼, 46½, 50¾, 55, 59¼)" (86.5 [96.5, 107.5, 118, 129, 139.5, 150.5] cm) bust circumference. Pullover shown measures 38" (96.5 cm).

yarn

Worsted weight (#4 Medium).

SHOWN HERE: Cascade Eco + (100% Peruvian wool; 478 yd [437 m]/ 250 g): #4010 straw, 3 (3, 3, 3, 4, 4, 4) skeins.

needles

BODY: size U.S. 7 (4.5 mm): 32" (80 cm) circular (cir) and set of 4 double-pointed (dpn).

RIBBING: size U.S. 5 (3.75 mm): 32" (80 cm) cir and set of 4 dpn.

Adjust needle size if necessary to obtain the correct gauge.

notions

Worsted-weight waste yarn for tubular CO; large stitch holders or waste yarn; markers (m); tapestry needle.

gauge

17 sts and 22 rnds = 4" (10 cm) in St st on larger needles, worked in rnds.

shaping set-in sleeves while working in rounds

Although set-in sleeves are most commonly knitted separately and sewn in place, it is possible to create set-in shaping while working a yoke in a single piece from the bottom up.

Begin with the stitches for the front(s), back, and sleeves on a circular needle with the underarm stitches on holders and markers denoting the boundaries between the pieces (**Figure 1**).

Decrease 1 stitch on the body side of each marker every row (or round) until the number of back stitches corresponds to the desired upper back width (**Figure 2**).

Shift each marker 1 stitch away from the center of each sleeve cap so that 2 body stitches (one each from front and back) are transferred to each sleeve. This maintains the alignment of the decreases from the armhole to the sleeve cap.

Dec 1 stitch on the sleeve side of each marker until about 2″ (5 cm) of sleeve stitches remain and the armhole is about 1″ (2.5 cm) less than the desired total length (**Figure 3**).

Shape the top of the cap by working back and forth in short-rows across the right front, back, and left front as follows (**Figure 4**):

Right Front: *With right side facing, work to marker, slip marker, work ssk decrease (see Glossary), turn work so wrong side is facing, slip 1, work to end; repeat from * until half of the sleeve cap stitches have been decreased (not counting the 1 extra body stitch at each marker), remove the marker after the last ssk. Do not turn work.

Back: With right side facing, work to last 2 sts of sleeve, *work k2tog decrease, slip marker, work to left back marker, slip marker, ssk, turn work so wrong side is facing, slip 1 purlwise with yarn in front, slip marker, work to right back marker, slip marker, slip 2 stitches purlwise with yarn in front, turn work; rep from * until the last 2 slipped sts of right back are the last stitches of the right sleeve.

With right side facing, k2tog, slip marker, work to left back marker, remove marker, ssk, work to 2 sts before left front marker, k2tog, slip marker, work to end.

Left Front: *With wrong side facing, work to left front marker, slip marker, slip 2 stitches purlwise with yarn in front, turn work so right side is facing, k2tog, work to end; rep from * until all sleeve stitches have been decreased (not counting the 1 extra body stitch at each marker).

With wrong side facing, *work to marker at shoulder, remove marker, slip 2 stitches purlwise with yarn in front (these are the remaining sleeve stitches); rep from * once more while binding off stitches for the back neck if desired, work to end.

Shoulders: Divide the stitches for each shoulder onto 2 double-pointed needles. Hold the needles parallel with right sides of knitting facing together and use the three-needle method (see Glossary) to bind off the stitches together. Bind off the remaining neck stitches if they haven't been bound off already.

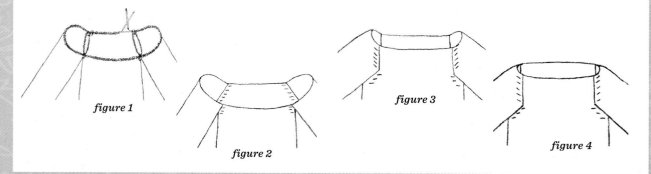

figure 1

figure 2

figure 3

figure 4

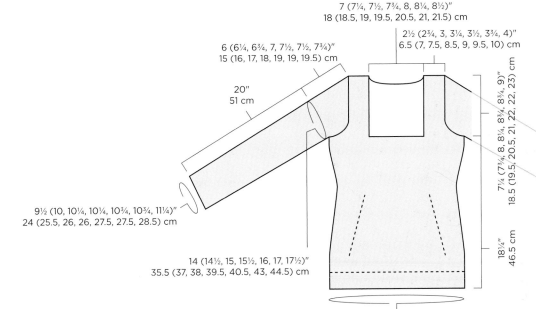

7 (7¼, 7½, 7¾, 8, 8¼, 8½)"
18 (18.5, 19, 19.5, 20.5, 21, 21.5) cm

2½ (2¾, 3, 3¼, 3½, 3¾, 4)"
6.5 (7, 7.5, 8.5, 9, 9.5, 10) cm

6 (6¼, 6¾, 7, 7½, 7½, 7¾)"
15 (16, 17, 18, 19, 19, 19.5) cm

20"
51 cm

7¼ (7¾, 8, 8¼, 8¾, 8¾, 9)"
18.5 (19.5, 20.5, 21, 22, 22, 23) cm

9½ (10, 10¼, 10¼, 10¾, 10¾, 11¼)"
24 (25.5, 26, 26, 27.5, 27.5, 28.5) cm

18¼"
46.5 cm

14 (14½, 15, 15½, 16, 17, 17½)"
35.5 (37, 38, 39.5, 40.5, 43, 44.5) cm

34 (38, 42¼, 46½, 50¾, 55, 59¼)"
86.5 (96.5, 107.5, 118, 129, 139.5, 150.5) cm

Sleeves

With smaller dpn, use the circular tubular method (see Glossary) to CO 54 (56, 58, 58, 60, 62, 64) sts. Arrange sts on 3 dpn, place marker (pm) and join for working in rnds, being careful not to twist sts.

SET-UP RND: *K1, p1; rep from *.

Cont in k1, p1 rib as established until piece measures 2" (5 cm) from CO.

DEC RND: [K2, k2tog] 13 (14, 14, 14, 14, 15, 16) times, [k2tog] 1 (0, 0, 0, 0, 1, 0) time, k0 (0, 2, 2, 4, 0, 0)—40 (42, 44, 44, 46, 46, 48) sts rem.

Change to larger dpn and work even in St st until piece measures 3" (7.5 cm) from CO.

INC RND: K1, M1 (see Glossary), knit to last st, M1, k1—2 sts inc'd.

Knit 9 (9, 9, 9, 9, 7, 7) rnds.

Rep the last 10 (10, 10, 10, 10, 8, 8) rnds 3 (4, 5, 1, 1, 6, 6) more time(s)—48 (52, 56, 48, 50, 60, 62) sts.

[Rep inc rnd, then knit 7 (7, 7, 7, 7, 5, 5) rnds] 6 (5, 4, 9, 9, 6, 6) times—60 (62, 64, 66, 68, 72, 74) sts.

Cont even in St st until piece measures 20" (51 cm) from CO, ending last rnd 4 (5, 6, 7, 8, 9, 10) sts before beg-of-rnd m.

Place the next 8 (10, 12, 14, 16, 18, 20) sts onto holder or waste yarn for underarm, removing marker. Place rem 52 (52, 52, 52, 52, 54, 54) sts onto waste yarn to be worked later.

Cut yarn and set aside. Make a second sleeve to match.

Body

With smaller cir needle, use the circular tubular method to CO 192 (216, 240, 264, 288, 312, 336) sts.

SET-UP RND: *K1, p1; rep from *.

Cont in k1, p1 rib as established until piece measures 2" (5 cm) from CO.

DEC RND: *K2tog, k2; rep from *—144 (162, 180, 198, 216, 234, 252) sts rem.

Pocket

Note: When establishing the pocket, the sts for the pocket are doubled by working 2 sts into each st (see sidebar on page 128). On the following row, the inc'd sts are placed onto a holder to be worked later with the body sts.

When slipping the sts onto the holder, move the yarn to the back (RS) and hold the holder in the front of the work (WS). The pocket sts are worked back and forth in rows, then placed onto a holder to be joined with the body later.

SET-UP ROW: With larger cir needle, k6 (9, 12, 15, 18, 21, 24), pm, [k1f&b (see Glossary)] 2 times, [p1f&b (see Glossary), k1f&b] 2 times, [k1f&b] 49 (52, 55, 58, 61, 64, 67) times, [p1f&b, k1f&b] 2 times, k1, pm, turn work, leaving rem 78 (90, 102, 114, 126, 138, 150) sts unworked.

Cont working back and forth between markers for pocket as foll:

NEXT ROW: (WS) Sl 1 purlwise with yarn in front (pwise wyf), [place 1 st onto holder, p1, place 1 st onto holder, k1] 2 times, *place 1 st onto holder, p1; rep from * to 6 sts before m, [place 1 st onto holder, k1, place 1 st onto holder, p1] 2 times, place 1 st onto holder, p1—59 (62, 65, 68, 71, 74, 77) body sts on holder; 60 (63, 66, 69, 72, 75, 78) pocket sts.

ROW 1: (RS) Sl 1 pwise with yarn in back (wyb), [k1, p1] 2 times, knit to last 5 sts, [p1, k1] 2 times, k1.

ROW 2: (WS) Sl 1 pwise wyf, [p1, k1] 2 times, purl to last 5 sts, [k1, p1] 2 times, p1.

Rep these 2 rows 4 more times.

DEC ROW 1: Sl 1 pwise wyb, [k1, p1] 2 times, k2tog, knit to last 7 sts, ssk, [p1, k1] 2 times, k1—2 sts dec'd.

Work 7 rows even as established.

Rep the last 8 rows 3 more times, then work the dec row once more—50 (53, 56, 59, 62, 65, 68) sts rem. Work 6 rows even, ending after a RS row.

DEC ROW 2: (WS) Sl 1 pwise wyb, [ssk] 2 times, knit to last 5 sts, [k2tog] 2 times, k1—46 (49, 52, 55, 58, 61, 64) sts rem.

Place 46 (49, 52, 55, 58, 61, 64) pocket sts onto holder or waste yarn, cut yarn, and set aside.

JOINING RND: (RS) Place 59 (62, 65, 68, 71, 74, 77) held body sts onto left needle tip. Remove pocket marker. Join yarn at the right-hand edge of the pocket and work as foll: M1, k29 (30, 32, 33, 35, 36, 38) sts, k2tog, k28 (30, 32, 33, 34, 36, 37) sts, remove pocket marker, M1, knit to end of rnd—144 (162, 180, 198, 216, 234, 252) sts total.

Knit 9 (9, 11, 11, 11, 13, 13) rnds.

Shape Waist and Join Pocket

SET-UP RND: *K1, k2tog, k66 (75, 84, 93, 102, 111, 120), ssk, k1, pm; rep from * once—140 (158, 176, 194, 212, 230, 248) sts rem.

Knit 9 rnds.

DEC RND: *K1, k2tog, knit to 3 sts before next m, ssk, k1, slip marker (sl m); rep from * once—4 sts dec'd.

Rep the last 10 rnds once—132 (150, 168, 186, 204, 222, 240) sts rem.

[Knit 7 rnds, then rep dec rnd] 2 times—124 (142, 160, 178, 196, 214, 232) sts rem.

Knit 5 (5, 3, 3, 3, 1, 1) rnd(s).

POCKET JOINING RND: K8 (11, 14, 17, 20, 23, 26), return 46 (49, 52, 55, 58, 61, 64) held pocket sts onto empty needle and hold in front of body sts, *k2tog (1 st from each pocket and body); rep from * until all pocket sts are joined, knit to end—still 124 (142, 160, 178, 196, 214, 232) sts.

Knit 7 rnds.

INC RND: *K1, M1, knit to 1 st before next m, M1, k1 sl m; rep from * once—4 sts inc'd.

Knit 5 rnds.

Rep the last 6 rnds 4 more times—144 (162, 180, 198, 216, 234, 252) sts.

Divide for Front Neck

K21 (25, 29, 33, 37, 41, 45), BO 30 (31, 32, 33, 34, 35, 36) sts, knit to end—114 (131, 148, 165, 182, 199, 216) sts rem.

Cut yarn.

Yoke

Slip 21 (25, 29, 33, 37, 41, 45) body sts onto the cir needle so that the needle tips are at the center front neck. Cont working back and forth in rows as foll:

JOINING ROW: With RS facing, join yarn at right front neck edge, work 16 (19, 22, 25, 28, 31, 34) right front sts, return one set of held sleeve sts onto dpn, k2tog (1 st from front with 1 st from sleeve), pm, place next 8 (10, 12, 14, 16, 18, 20) body sts onto holder or waste yarn for underarm, work 50 (50, 50, 50, 50, 52, 52) sleeve sts, pm, ssk (1 st from sleeve with next st from body), work 62 (69, 76, 83,

90, 97, 104) back sts, return sts of other sleeve onto dpn, k2tog (1 st from back with 1 st from sleeve), pm, place next 8 (10, 12, 14, 16, 18, 20) body sts onto holder or waste yarn for underarm, work 50 (50, 50, 50, 50, 52, 52) sleeve sts, pm, ssk (1 st from sleeve with next st from body), work 16 (19, 22, 25, 28, 31, 34) front sts—198 (211, 224, 237, 250, 267, 280) sts total.

Shape Armholes

DEC ROW 1: (WS) *Work to 2 sts before m, ssp (see Glossary), sl m, work to next m, sl m, p2tog; rep from * once, work to end—4 body sts dec'd.

DEC ROW 2: (RS) *Work to 2 sts before m, k2tog, sl m, work to next m, sl m, ssk; rep from * once, work to end—4 body sts dec'd.

Rep the last 2 rows 1 (2, 3, 4, 5, 7, 8) more time(s), for a total of 4 (6, 8, 10, 12, 16, 18) rows, ending after a RS row—182 (187, 192, 197, 202, 203, 208) sts rem; 13 (14, 15, 16, 17, 16, 17) sts for each front, 50 (50, 50, 50, 50, 52, 52) sts for each sleeve, 56 (59, 62, 65, 68, 67, 70) sts for back.

[Purl 1 WS row, then rep Dec Row 2] 2 (2, 2, 2, 2, 0, 0) times—174 (179, 184, 189, 194, 203, 208) sts rem; 11 (12, 13, 14, 15, 16, 17) sts for each front, 50 (50, 50, 50, 50, 52, 52) sts for each sleeve, 52 (55, 58, 61, 64, 67, 70) sts for back.

Shape Sleeve Caps

SET-UP ROW: (WS) *Purl to 1 st before m, sl 1 pwise, remove m, replace slipped st back onto left needle tip, replace m, purl to next m, remove m, p1, replace m; rep from * once, work to end—still 174 (179, 184, 189, 194, 203, 208) sts; 10 (11, 12, 13, 14, 15, 16) sts for each front; 52 (52, 52, 52, 52, 54, 54) sts for each sleeve; 50 (53, 56, 59, 62, 65, 68) sts for back.

DEC ROW 1: (RS) *Work to m, sl m, ssk, work to 2 sts before next m, k2tog, sl m; rep from * once, work to end—2 sts dec'd each sleeve.

Work 1 WS row even.

Rep the last 2 rows 2 (2, 2, 2, 2, 1, 1) more time(s)—162 (167, 172, 177, 182, 195, 200) sts rem; 46 (46, 46, 46, 46, 50, 50) sts for each sleeve.

Rep Dec Row 1—2 sts dec'd each sleeve.

DEC ROW 2: (WS) *Work to m, sl m, p2tog, work to 2 sts before next m, ssp, sl m; rep from * once, work to end—2 sts dec'd each sleeve.

Rep the last 2 rows (i.e., dec every row) 8 (8, 8, 8, 8, 9, 9) more times—90 (95, 100, 105, 110, 115, 120) sts rem; 10 (11, 12, 13, 14, 15, 16) sts for each front, 10 sts for each sleeve, 50 (53, 56, 59, 62, 65, 68) sts for back.

Shape top of cap and back neck with short-rows (see Glossary) as foll:

Note: Sts on sleeves are not wrapped when turning, but sts at the neck edges are wrapped.

SHORT-ROW 1: With RS facing, knit to m, sl m, ssk, turn work so WS is facing, sl 1 pwise wyf, sl m, knit to end—1 st dec'd.

Rep Short-Row 1 two more times.

SHORT-ROW 2: With RS facing, work to m, remove m, ssk, work to 2 sts before next m, k2tog, sl m, work 20 (21, 22, 23, 24, 25, 26) sts, wrap next st, turn work so WS is facing, work to m, sl m, sl 2 sts pwise wyf, turn work—2 sts dec'd.

SHORT-ROW 3: With RS facing, k2tog, sl m, work 17 (18, 19, 20, 21, 22, 23) sts, wrap next st and turn work so WS is facing, work to m, sl m, sl 2 sts pwise wyf, turn work—1 st dec'd.

SHORT-ROW 4: With RS facing, k2tog, sl m, work 15 (16, 17, 18, 19, 20, 21) sts, wrap next st, turn work so WS is facing, work to m, sl m, sl 2 sts pwise wyf, turn work—1 st dec'd.

SHORT-ROW 5: With RS facing, k2tog, sl m, work to next m hiding wraps as they appear, sl m, ssk, turn work so WS is facing, sl 1 pwise wyf, sl m, work 20 (21, 22, 23, 24, 25, 26) sts, wrap next st, turn work—2 sts dec'd.

SHORT-ROW 6: With RS facing, work to m, sl m, ssk, turn work so WS is facing, sl 1 pwise wyf, sl m, work 17 (18, 19, 20, 21, 22, 23) sts—1 st dec'd.

SHORT-ROW 7: With RS facing, work to m, sl m, ssk, turn work so WS is facing, sl 1 pwise wyf, sl m, work 15 (16, 17, 18, 19, 20, 21) sts—1 st dec'd.

SHORT-ROW 8: With RS facing, work to m, remove m, ssk, work to 2 sts before next m, k2tog, sl m, work to end—2 sts dec'd.

SHORT-ROW 9: With WS facing, work to m, sl m, sl 2 sts pwise wyf, turn work so RS is facing, k2tog, sl m, work to end—1 st dec'd.

Rep the last short-row 2 more times—74 (79, 84, 89, 94, 99, 104) sts rem.

NEXT ROW: (WS) Work to m, remove m, sl 2 sts pwise wyf, sl m, work 10 (11, 12, 13, 14, 15, 16) sts, BO center 30 (31, 32, 33, 34, 35, 36) sts for back neck hiding wraps as they appear, work to next m, remove m, sl 2 sts pwise wyf, work to end—22 (24, 26, 28, 30, 32, 34) sts rem each side for shoulders.

Divide sts on each shoulder in half onto 2 larger dpn. Hold the needles parallel with RS facing tog and use the three-needle method (see Glossary) to BO sts tog.

Collar

With smaller cir needle, RS facing, and beg at right front corner of neck BO, pick up and knit 116 (120, 126, 130, 136, 138, 142) sts evenly spaced (about 1 st in each row along neck edge to shoulder, 1 st in shoulder seam, 1 st in each back neck BO st, 1 st in each row along neck edge to front neck BO sts, and 1 st in first front neck BO st) around neck opening.

ROW 1: (WS) Ssk, p1, *k1, p1; rep from * to last st, sl 1 pwise wyf.

ROW 2: (RS) Pick up and knit 1 st in the back loop of the nearest front BO st and place the st onto the left needle tip, p2tog, k1, *p1, k1; rep from * to last st, sl 1 pwise wyb, [pick up and knit 1 st in the back loop of next front BO st] 2 times.

ROW 3: Sssk (see Glossary), p1, *k1, p1; rep from * to last st, sl 1 st pwise wyf.

ROW 4: [Pick up and knit 1 st in the back loop of the nearest front BO st and place the st onto the left needle tip] 2 times, p3tog, k1, *p1, k1; rep from * to last st, sl 1 pwise wyb, pick up and knit 1 st in the back loop of next front BO st.

Rep the last 4 rows 3 (3, 4, 4, 4, 4, 4) more times.

Cont for your size as foll.

Sizes 34 (38, 59¼)" only
Pick up and knit 1 st in the back loop of the next front BO st (2 sts picked up total).

ROW 5: (WS) Sssk, p1, *k1, p1; rep from * to last st, sl 1 pwise wyf.

ROW 6: (RS) [Pick up and knit 1 st in the back loop of the nearest front BO st and place the st onto the left needle tip] 2 times, p3tog, k1, *p1, k1; rep from * to last st, sl 1 pwise wyb, pick up and knit 1 st in the back loop of next front BO st.

Sizes 50¾ (55)" only
Rep Rows 1 and 2, picking up only 1 st at the end of Row 2.

All sizes
Shape collar with short-rows as foll:

SHORT-ROW 1: With WS facing, ssk, *p1, k1; rep from * to last 8 sts, wrap next st, turn work so RS is facing, p1, *k1, p1; rep from * to last 8 sts, wrap next st, turn work.

SHORT-ROW 2: With WS facing, k1, *p1, k1; rep from * to 4 sts before wrapped st, wrap next st, turn work so RS is facing, p1, *k1, p1; rep from * to 4 sts before wrapped st, wrap next st, turn work.

SHORT-ROW 3: With WS facing, k1, *p1, k1; rep from * to 2 sts before wrapped st, wrap next st, turn work so RS is facing, p1, *k1, p1; rep from * to 2 sts before wrapped st, wrap next st, turn work.

Rep Short-Row 3 twice more, then work Short-Row 2 once again.

NEXT SHORT-ROW: With WS facing, k1, *p1, k1; rep from * to 6 sts before wrapped st, wrap next st, turn work so RS is facing, p1, *k1, p1; rep from * to 6 sts before wrapped st, wrap next st, turn work.

Rep the last short-row 2 more times.

NEXT ROW: (WS) *K1, p1; rep from * to last st, hiding wraps as they appear, sl 1 pwise wyf.

Cont for your size as foll.

Sizes 34 (42¼, 50¾, 59¼)" only

NEXT ROW: (RS) Pick up and knit 1 st in the back loop of the nearest front BO st and place the st onto the left needle tip, cont binding off as foll: p2tog, *k1, p1; rep from * to end, hiding wraps as they appear.

Sizes 38 (46½, 55)" only

NEXT ROW: (RS) Pick up and knit 1 st in the back loop of the nearest front BO st and place the st onto the left needle tip, p2tog, k1, *p1, k1; rep from * to last st, hiding wraps as they appear, sl 1 st pwise wyb.

NEXT ROW: (WS) Pick up and knit 1 st in the back loop of the next front BO st, cont binding off as foll: p2tog, *k1, p1; rep from * to end.

Finishing

Turn garment inside out. Place held underarm sts onto smaller dpn, pick up 1 st at each end of each dpn to prevent a hole from forming. Hold the needles parallel with RS facing tog and use the three-needle method to BO the sts tog.

Weave in loose ends. Block to measurements (see Glossary).

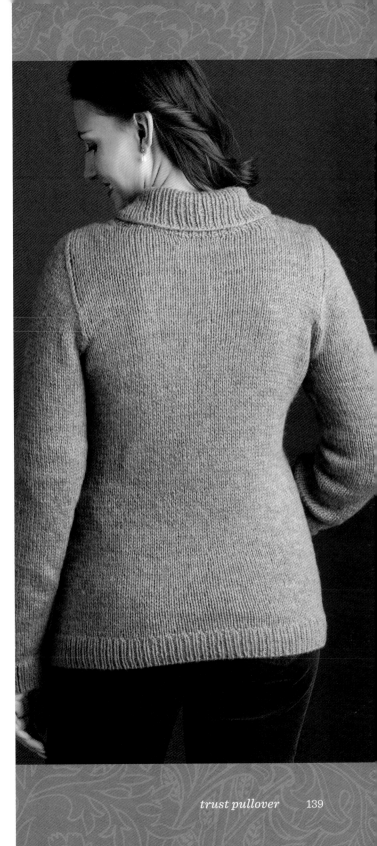

beauty ✿ CARDI

The beauty of Beauty is its seamless set-in sleeve construction. The body and sleeves, which are worked separately to the armholes, begin with a bit of lace followed by broken ribs. The yoke is shaped with decreases worked on the body to draw in the armholes, then the sleeve stitches are decreased to shape the caps. A few short-rows are worked to finish the caps and shape the neck, then the shoulders are joined with a three-needle bind-off.

Finished Size

About 31½ (36, 40½, 44¾, 49¼, 53½, 58)" (80 [91.5, 103, 113.5, 125, 136, 147.5] cm) bust circumference with 1" (2.5 cm) overlap.

Cardigan shown measures 36" (91.5 cm).

Yarn

Worsted weight (#4 Medium).

SHOWN HERE: Classic Elite Solstice (70% organic cotton, 30% merino; 100 yd [91 m]/50 g): #2346 faded teal, 9 (10, 11, 13, 14, 15, 17) skeins.

Needles

Size U.S. 5 (3.75 mm): 32" (80 cm) circular (cir) and set of 4 double-pointed (dpn).

Adjust needle size if necessary to obtain the correct gauge.

Notions

Stitch holders or waste yarn; markers (m); one 1" (2.5 cm) button; tapestry needle.

Gauge

20 sts and 28 rows = 4" (10 cm) in garter rib patt.

Body

With circular needle, use the long-tail method (see Glossary) to CO 162 (184, 206, 228, 250, 272, 294) sts. Do not join.

Working back and forth in rows, knit 2 rows, ending after a WS row.

Beg and end as indicated for rows, work Rows 1–12 of Lace chart 2 times.

Rep Rows 1 and 2 of Garter Rib chart until piece measures 14½ (14¾, 15, 15¼, 15½, 15¾, 16)" (37 [37.5, 38, 38.5, 39.5, 40, 40.5] cm) from CO, ending after a RS row.

Cont for your size as foll:

Sizes 31½ (40½, 49¼, 58)" only

DEC RND: Work 37 (46, 56, 66) sts, pm for underarm, work 4 (6, 7, 8) sts, k2tog, work 5 (7, 8, 9) sts, pm, work 66 (84, 104, 124) sts, pm for underarm, work 4 (6, 7, 8) sts, k2tog, work 5 (7, 8, 9) sts, pm, work to end—160 (204, 248, 292) sts rem.

Sizes 36 (44¾, 53½)" only

Work 42 (51, 61) sts, pm for underarm, work 12 (16, 18) sts, pm, work 76 (94, 114) sts, pm for underarm, work 12 (16, 18) sts, pm, work to end—still 184 (228, 272) sts.

All sizes

Leave sts on cir needle, do not cut yarn. Set aside.

☐	knit on RS; purl on WS
·	purl on RS; knit on WS
∕	k2tog
∖	ssk
o	yo
▯	pattern repeat

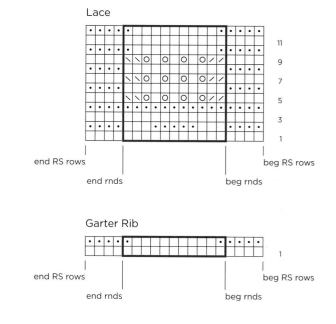

Lace

Garter Rib

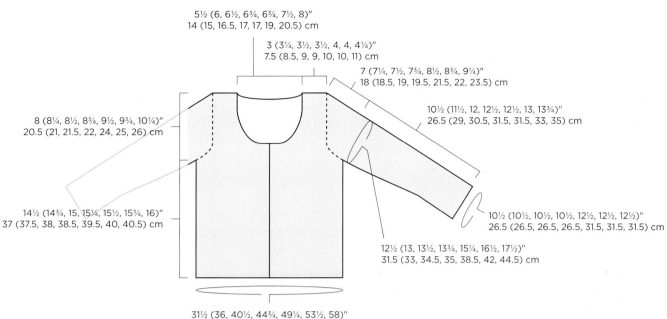

5½ (6, 6½, 6¾, 6¾, 7½, 8)"
14 (15, 16.5, 17, 17, 19, 20.5) cm

3 (3¼, 3½, 3½, 4, 4, 4¼)"
7.5 (8.5, 9, 9, 10, 10, 11) cm

7 (7¼, 7½, 7¾, 8½, 8¾, 9¼)"
18 (18.5, 19, 19.5, 21.5, 22, 23.5) cm

8 (8¼, 8½, 8¾, 9½, 9¾, 10¼)"
20.5 (21, 21.5, 22, 24, 25, 26) cm

10½ (11½, 12, 12½, 12½, 13, 13¾)"
26.5 (29, 30.5, 31.5, 31.5, 33, 35) cm

14½ (14¾, 15, 15¼, 15½, 15¾, 16)"
37 (37.5, 38, 38.5, 39.5, 40, 40.5) cm

10½ (10½, 10½, 10½, 12½, 12½, 12½)"
26.5 (26.5, 26.5, 26.5, 31.5, 31.5, 31.5) cm

12½ (13, 13½, 13¾, 15¼, 16½, 17½)"
31.5 (33, 34.5, 35, 38.5, 42, 44.5) cm

31½ (36, 40½, 44¾, 49¼, 53½, 58)"
80 (91.5, 103, 113.5, 125, 136, 147.5) cm
with 1" (2.5 cm) buttonband overlapped

Sleeves

CO 55 (55, 55, 55, 66, 66, 66) sts. Divide onto dpn in multiples of 11 sts on each needle. Being careful not to twist sts, join for working a purl rnd (see Glossary) so that the joining bump is on the RS. Place marker (pm) to denote beg of rnd. Knit 1 rnd, then purl 1 rnd.

Work Rnds 1–12 of Lace chart 2 times.

Change to garter rib chart and cont as foll:

INC RND: K1, M1 (see Glossary), work in patt to last st, M1, k1—2 sts inc'd.

Inc 1 st each side of m in this manner every 12 (10, 10, 8, 12, 8, 8) rnds 1 (2, 1, 4, 2, 3, 2) more time(s), then every 10 (8, 8, 6, 10, 6, 6) rnds 1 (2, 3, 2, 2, 3, 2) time(s), then every 8 (0, 6, 0, 0, 4, 4) rnds 1 (0, 1, 0, 0, 1, 6) time(s), working inc'd sts into patt as they become available—63 (65, 67, 69, 76, 82, 88) sts.

Cont even as established until piece measures 10½ (11½, 12, 12½, 12½, 13, 13¾)" (26.5 [29, 30.5, 31.5, 31.5, 33, 35] cm) from CO, ending after working Rnd 2 of rib patt 5 (6, 7, 8, 8, 9, 9) sts before the beg-of-rnd m.

Place the next 10 (12, 14, 16, 16, 18, 18) sts onto holder or waste yarn for underarm, removing marker. Place rem 53 (53, 53, 53, 60, 64, 70) sts onto waste yarn to be worked later. Cut yarn.

Yoke

JOINING RND: With RS facing and cont in patt as established, work 36 (41, 45, 50, 55, 60, 65) front sts, k2tog (1 front st with 1 sleeve st), pm for underarm, place next 10 (12, 14, 16, 16, 18, 18) body sts onto holder or waste yarn for underarm, work 51 (51, 51, 51, 58, 62, 68) sleeve sts, pm for underarm, ssk (1 sleeve st with 1 body st), work 64 (74, 82, 92, 102, 112, 122) back sts, k2tog (1 back st with 1 sleeve st, pm for underarm, place next 10 (12, 14, 16, 16, 18, 18) body sts onto holder or waste yarn for underarm, work 51 (51, 51, 51, 58, 62, 68) sleeve sts, pm for underarm, ssk (1 sleeve st with 1 body st), work 36 (41, 45, 50, 55, 60, 65) front sts—242 (262, 278, 298, 332, 360, 392) sts total.

Shape Armholes

DEC ROW 1: (WS) *Work to 2 sts before m, ssp (see Glossary), sl m, work to next m, sl m, p2tog; rep from * once more, work to end—4 body sts dec'd.

DEC ROW 2: (RS) *Work to 2 sts before m, k2tog, sl m, work to next m, sl m, ssk; rep from * once more, work to end—4 body sts dec'd.

Rep the last 2 rows 0 (2, 3, 4, 6, 7, 9) more times, for a total of 2 (6, 8, 10, 14, 16, 20) rows, ending after a RS row.

Cont for your size as foll:

Sizes 31½ (44¾, 53½)" only
Work 1 WS row even, then rep Dec Row 2 once more.

All sizes
There will rem 230 (238, 246, 254, 276, 292, 312) sts; 34 (36, 38, 40, 42, 44, 46) sts for each front, 51 (51, 51, 51, 58, 62, 68) sts for each sleeve; 60 (64, 68, 72, 76, 80, 84) sts for back.

Shape Sleeve Cap

SET-UP ROW: (WS) Keeping in patt, *work to 1 st before m, sl 1 pwise, remove m, return slipped st onto left needle tip, replace m, work to next m, remove m, work 1 st, replace m; rep from * once, work to end—33 (35, 37, 39, 41, 43, 45) sts for each front; 53 (53, 53, 53, 60, 64, 70) sts for each sleeve; 58 (62, 66, 70, 74, 78, 82) sts for back.

BUTTONHOLE AND DEC ROW: (RS) K2, [yo] 2 times, k2tog, *work in patt to m, sl m, ssk, work to 2 sts before next m, k2tog, sl m; rep from * once, work to end—1 buttonhole made; 2 sts dec'd each sleeve.

NEXT ROW: Keeping in patt, work to double yo, knit into first wrap of double yo and drop second wrap, work to end.

CAP DEC ROW 1: (RS) On the first row only, work 2 sts, work the next st into the double yo from 2 rows below; for first row and all reps of dec row, work as foll: *work to m, sl m, ssk, work to 2 sts before next m, k2tog, sl m; rep from * once, work to end—2 sts dec'd each sleeve.

Cont for your size as foll:

Sizes 31½ (36, 40½, 44¾, 49¼)" only
Work 1 WS row even.

Rep the last 2 rows once more.

Sizes 53½ (58)" only

CAP DEC ROW 2: (WS) Keeping in patt, *work to m, sl m, p2tog, work to 2 sts before next m, ssp, sl m; rep from * once, work to end—2 sts dec'd each sleeve.

Rep the last 2 rows once more.

All sizes
There will rem 218 (226, 234, 242, 264, 272, 292) sts; 33 (35, 37, 39, 41, 43, 45) sts for each front; 47 (47, 47, 47, 54, 54, 60) sts for each sleeve; 58 (62, 66, 70, 74, 78, 82) sts for back.

Note: Neck shaping begins while sleeve cap shaping is in progress; read all the way through the foll sections before proceeding.

Work Cap Dec Row 1 on next RS row, then cont to dec every other row 7 (7, 7, 5, 3, 1, 0) time(s), then dec every row 11 (11, 11, 13, 19, 21, 25) times, working WS dec rows as Cap Dec Row 2, described for sizes 53½ (58)" above and *at the same time* on the first RS row shape front neck as foll.

Shape Front Neck

(RS) Cont working sleeve cap shaping as established, BO 7 (7, 7, 7, 7, 8, 8) sts at beg of next 2 rows, then BO 3 (3, 3, 3, 3, 3, 4) sts at beg of next 2 rows—23 (25, 27, 29, 31, 32, 33) sts rem for each front.

NECK DEC ROW 1: (RS) K1, k2tog, work to last 3 sts, ssk, k1—1 st dec'd each front.

NECK DEC ROW 2: (WS) P1, ssp, work to last 3 sts, p2tog, p1—1 st dec'd each front.

Rep Neck Dec Row 1 on next RS row, then every other row 5 (6, 7, 8, 8, 9, 9) more times—15 (16, 17, 18, 20, 20, 21) sts rem for each front.

Cont working sleeve cap shaping as specified, ending after the last WS dec row—106 (112, 118, 124, 130, 134, 140) sts rem; 15 (16, 17, 18, 20, 20, 21) sts for each front, 9 (9, 9, 9, 8, 8, 8) sts for each sleeve, 58 (62, 66, 70, 74, 78, 82) sts for back.

Shape Top of Cap

Note: Sleeve sts are not wrapped when working short-rows, but neck edge sts are wrapped.

Work short-rows (see Glossary) as foll:

SHORT-ROW 1: With RS facing, work to m, sl m, ssk, turn work so WS is facing, sl 1 pwise wyf, sl m, work to end—1 st dec'd.

Rep this short-row 2 (2, 2, 2, 1, 1, 1) more time(s).

SHORT-ROW 2: With RS facing, work to m, remove m, ssk, work to 2 sts before next m, k2tog, sl m, work 23 (24, 25, 26, 28, 28, 29) sts, wrap next st, turn work so WS is facing, work to m, sl m, sl 2 sts pwise wyf, turn work—2 sts dec'd.

SHORT-ROW 3: With RS facing, k2tog, sl m, work 18 (19, 20, 21, 23, 23, 24) sts, wrap next st, turn work so WS is facing, work to m, sl m, sl 2 sts pwise wyf, turn work—1 st dec'd.

SHORT-ROW 4: With RS facing, k2tog, sl m, work to next m hiding wraps as they appear, sl m, ssk, turn work so WS is

facing, sl 1 pwise wyf, sl m, work 23 (24, 25, 26, 28, 28, 29) sts, wrap next st, turn work—2 sts dec'd.

SHORT-ROW 5: With RS facing, work to m, sl m, ssk, turn work so WS is facing, sl 1 pwise wyf, sl m, work 18 (19, 20, 21, 23, 23, 24) sts, wrap next st, turn work—1 st dec'd.

SHORT-ROW 6: With RS facing, work to m, remove m, ssk, work to 2 sts before next m, k2tog, sl m, work to end—2 sts dec'd.

SHORT-ROW 7: With WS facing, work to m, sl m, sl 2 sts pwise wyf, turn work so RS is facing, k2tog, sl m, work to end—1 st dec'd.

Rep the last short-row 2 (2, 2, 2, 1, 1, 1) more time(s).

NEXT ROW: (WS) Work to m, remove m, sl 2 sts pwise wyf, work 15 (16, 17, 18, 20, 20, 21) sts, BO center 28 (30, 32, 34, 34, 38, 40) sts for back neck, work to next m, remove m, sl 2 sts pwise wyf, work to end—32 (34, 36, 38, 42, 42, 44) sts rem each side.

Divide sts on each shoulder in half onto 2 dpns. Hold needles parallel with RS facing tog and use the three-needle method (see Glossary) to BO sts tog so seam is on WS of work.

Finishing

Place each set of held underarm sts onto a separate dpn, picking up 1 additional st at each end of each needle. Hold needles parallel with RS facing tog and use the three-needle method to BO sts tog. Rep for other underarm.

Collar

With cir needle, RS facing, and beg at right front neck edge, pick up and knit 94 (96, 98, 98, 100, 100, 110) sts evenly spaced (1 st in each BO st and about 3 sts for every 4 rows) around neck edge.

NEXT ROW: (WS) Knit and *at the same time* dec 1 (inc 2, dec 0, dec 0, dec 2, inc 8, dec 2) sts evenly spaced—93 (98, 98, 98, 98, 108, 108) sts. Pm each side of center 31 (32, 34, 36, 38, 42, 42) sts. Work short-rows as foll:

SHORT-ROW 1: With RS facing, knit to second m, sl m, wrap next st, turn work so WS is facing, sl m, knit to next m, sl m, wrap next st, turn work.

SHORT-ROW 2: With RS facing, knit to wrapped st, knit wrapped st, k5, wrap next st, turn work so WS is facing, knit to wrapped st, knit wrapped st, k5, wrap next st, turn work.

Rep the last short-row 3 more times.

NEXT ROW: (RS) Knit to end.

INC ROW: With WS facing, k7, M1, *k5, M1; rep from * to last 6 sts, knit to end—110 (116, 116, 116, 116, 128, 128) sts total.

SHORT-ROW 3: With RS facing, p1, *p2, k2, p2; rep from * to last 7 sts, p1, wrap next st, turn work so WS is facing, knit to last 6 sts, wrap next st, turn work.

SHORT-ROW 4: With RS facing, cont in rib as established to 6 sts before wrapped st, wrap next st, turn so WS is facing, knit to 6 sts before wrapped st, wrap next st, turn work.

Rep the last short-row 2 more times.

SHORT-ROW 5: With RS facing, cont in rib as established to 3 sts before wrapped st, wrap next st, turn work so WS is facing, knit to 3 sts before wrapped st, wrap next st, turn work.

Rep the last short-row 4 more times.

NEXT ROW: (RS) Work to end in rib as established, hiding wraps as they appear.

Knit 2 rows, hiding the wraps as they appear on the first row, ending after a RS row. With WS facing, BO all sts kwise.

Sew button to left front opposite buttonhole. Weave in loose ends. Tack down collar at front edges if desired. Block to measurements (see Glossary).

GLOSSARY

Abbreviations

beg(s)	begin(s); beginning	M1	make one (increase)
BO	bind off	oz	ounce
cir	circular	p	purl
cm	centimeter(s)	p1f&b	purl into front and back of same stitch
cn	cable needle		
CO	cast on	p2tog	purl 2 stitches together
cont	continue(s); continuing	patt(s)	pattern(s)
dec(s)('d)	decrease(s); decreasing; decreased	pm	place marker
		psso	pass slipped stitch over
dpn	double-pointed needles	pwise	purlwise; as if to purl
foll(s)	follow(s); following	rem	remain(s); remaining
g	gram(s)	rep	repeat(s); repeating
inc(s)('d)	increase(s); increasing; increase(d)	Rev St st	reverse stockinette stitch
		rnd(s)	round(s)
k	knit	RS	right side
k1f&b	knit into the front and back of same stitch	sl	slip
		sl st	slip st (slip stitch purlwise unless otherwise indicated)
k2tog	knit 2 stitches together		
k3tog	knit 3 stitches together	ssk	ssk (decrease)
kwise	knitwise, as if to knit	st(s)	stitch(es)
m	marker(s)	St st	stockinette stitch
mm	millimeter(s)		

tbl	through back loop
tog	together
WS	wrong side
wyb	with yarn in back
wyf	with yarn in front
yd	yard(s)
yo	yarnover
*	repeat starting point
* *	repeat all instructions between asterisks
( )	alternate measurements and/or instructions
[ ]	work instructions as a group a specified number of times

Bind-Offs

Standard Bind-Off

Knit the first stitch, *knit the next stitch (two stitches on right needle), insert left needle tip into first stitch on right needle (**Figure 1**) and lift this stitch up and over the second stitch (**Figure 2**) and off the needle (**Figure 3**). Repeat from * for the desired number of stitches.

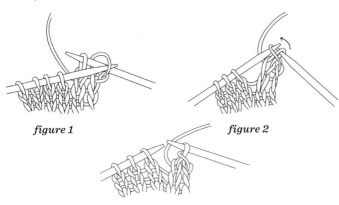

figure 1 *figure 2*

figure 3

Three-Needle Bind-Off

Place the stitches to be joined onto two separate needles and hold the needles parallel so that the right sides of knitting face together. Insert a third needle into the first stitch on each of two needles (**Figure 1**) and knit them together as one stitch (**Figure 2**), *knit the next stitch on each needle the same way, then use the left needle tip to lift the first stitch over the second and off the needle (**Figure 3**). Repeat from * until no stitches remain on first two needles. Cut yarn and pull tail through last stitch to secure.

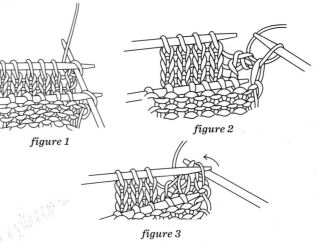

figure 1 *figure 2*

figure 3

Blocking

Steam Blocking

Pin the pieces to be blocked to a blocking surface. Hold an iron set on the steam setting ½″ (1.3 cm) above the knitted surface and direct the steam over the entire surface (except ribbing). You can get similar results by lapping wet cheesecloth on top of the knitted surface and touching it lightly with a dry iron. Lift and set down the iron gently; do not use a pushing motion.

Wet-Towel Blocking

Run a large bath or beach towel (or two towels for larger projects) through the rinse/spin cycle of a washing machine. Roll the knitted pieces in the wet towel(s), place the roll in a plastic bag, and leave overnight so that the knitted pieces become uniformly damp. Pin the damp pieces to a blocking surface and let air-dry thoroughly.

Buttons

To attach buttons, place a removable stitch marker in the fabric at each button location. Thread an 8″ (20.5 cm) length of yarn onto a tapestry needle. Secure one end of the yarn to the wrong side of the fabric, beginning a few stitches away from the marked button position and working toward the marker. Remove the marker, *bring the tapestry needle from the wrong side to the right side of the fabric, through one hole in the button, then back through another hole in the button, and into the fabric one or two stitches away from where it entered. Repeat from * two or three times. To finish, secure the remaining yarn on the wrong side of the fabric.

Cast-Ons

Backward-Loop Cast-On

*Loop working yarn and place it on needle backward so that it doesn't unwind. Repeat from *.

Cable Cast-On

If there are no stitches on the needles, make a slipknot of working yarn and place it on the left needle, then use the knitted method to cast-on one more stitch—two stitches on needle. When there are at least two stitches on the left needle, hold needle with working yarn in your left hand. *Insert right needle between the first two stitches on left needle (**Figure 1**), wrap yarn around needle as if to knit, draw yarn through (**Figure 2**), and place new loop on left needle (**Figure 3**) to form a new stitch. Repeat from * for the desired number of stitches, always working between the first two stitches on the left needle.

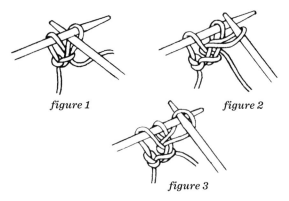

figure 1

figure 2

figure 3

Circular Tubular Cast-On for K1, P1 Rib

With waste yarn and circular or double-pointed needles, use desired method to cast on half the desired number of stitches. Join for working in rounds, being careful not to twist the stitches. Knit two rounds even. Change to working yarn and knit four more rounds.

NEXT RND: (RS) K1, *holding the yarn in front, use a needle tip to pick up the lowermost working yarn loop (forms a "dashed" line below the last round of waste yarn stitches) between the first two stitches (**Figure 1**), place this loop on the left needle tip, and purl it (**Figure 2**). Repeat from * to the end of the round. After working a few rounds in ribbing, cut out waste yarn.

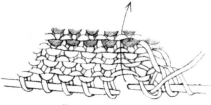

figure 1

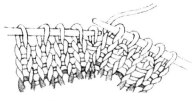

figure 2

Crochet Provisional Cast-On

With waste yarn and crochet hook, make a loose crochet chain (see page 152) about four stitches more than you need to cast on. With knitting needle, working yarn, and beginning two stitches from end of chain, pick up and knit one stitch through the back loop of each crochet chain (**Figure 1**) for desired number of stitches. When you're ready to work in the opposite direction, pull out the crochet chain to expose live stitches (**Figure 2**).

Knitted Cast-On

If there are no stitches on the needles, make a slipknot of working yarn and place it on the left needle. When there is at least one stitch on the left needle, *use the right needle to knit the first stitch (or slipknot) on left needle (**Figure 1**) and place new loop onto left needle to form a new stitch (**Figure 2**). Repeat from * for the desired number of stitches, always working into the last stitch made.

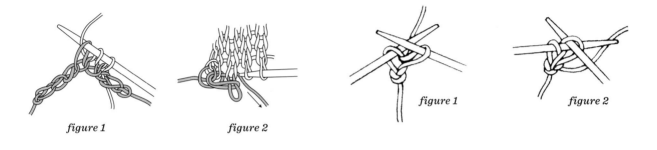

figure 1   *figure 2*   *figure 1*   *figure 2*

Long-Tail (Continental) Cast-On

Leaving a long tail (about ½" [1.3 cm] for each stitch to be cast on), make a slipknot and place on right needle. Place thumb and index finger of your left hand between the yarn ends so that working yarn is around your index finger and tail end is around your thumb and secure the yarn ends with your other fingers. Hold your palm upward, making a V of yarn (**Figure 1**). *Bring needle up through loop on thumb (**Figure 2**), catch first strand around index finger, and go back down through loop on thumb (**Figure 3**). Drop loop off thumb and, placing thumb back in V configuration, tighten resulting stitch on needle (**Figure 4**). Repeat from * for the desired number of stitches.

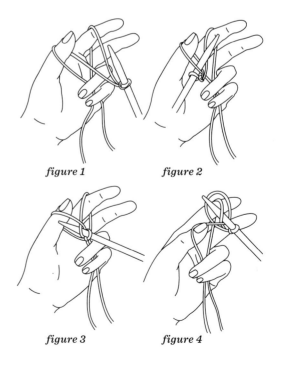

figure 1   *figure 2*

figure 3   *figure 4*

Crochet

Crochet Chain (ch)

Make a slipknot and place on crochet hook. *Yarn over hook and draw through a loop on the hook. Repeat from * for the desired number of stitches. To fasten off, cut yarn and draw end through last loop formed.

Decreases

Knit 2 Together (k2tog)

Knit two stitches together as if they were a single stitch.

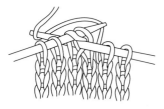

Knit 3 Together (k3tog)

Knit three stitches together as if they were a single stitch.

Slip, Slip, Knit (ssk)

Slip two stitches individually knitwise (**Figure 1**), insert left needle tip into the front of these two slipped stitches, and use the right needle to knit them together through their back loops (**Figure 2**).

Purl 2 Together (p2tog)

Purl two stitches together as if they were a single stitch.

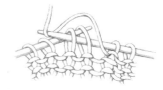

Purl 3 Together (p3tog)

Purl three stitches together as if they were a single stitch.

Slip, Slip, Slip, Knit (sssk)

Slip three stitches individually knitwise, insert left needle tip into the front of these three slipped stitches, and use the right needle to knit them together through their back loops.

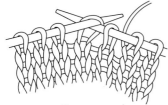
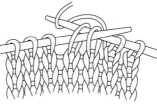

figure 1   *figure 2*

Slip, Slip, Purl (ssp)

Holding yarn in front, slip two stitches individually knit-wise (**Figure 1**), then slip these two stitches back onto left needle (they will be twisted on the needle), and purl them together through their back loops (**Figure 2**).

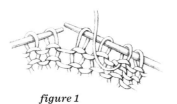
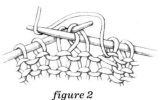

figure 1   *figure 2*

Joining for Working in Rounds

For projects that begin with ribbing or stockinette st, simply arrange the stitches for working in rounds, then knit the first stitch that was cast-on to form a tube.

For projects that begin with seed, garter, or reverse stockinette st, arrange the needle so that the yarn tail is at the left needle tip. Holding the yarn in back, slip the first st from the right needle onto the left needle (**Figure 1**), bring the yarn to the front between the two needles, and slip the first two stitches from the left tip to the right tip (**Figure 2**), then bring the yarn to the back between the two needles and slip the first stitch from the right tip to the left tip (**Figure 3**).

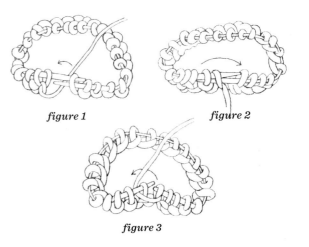

figure 1   *figure 2*

figure 3

Gauge

Measuring Gauge

Knit a swatch at least 4″ (10 cm) square. Remove the stitches from the needles or bind them off loosely and lay the swatch on a flat surface. Place a ruler over the swatch and count the number of stitches across and number of rows down (including fractions of stitches and rows) in 4″ (10 cm) and divide this number by four to get the number of stitches (including fractions of stitches) in one inch. Repeat two or three times on different areas of the swatch to confirm the measurements. If you have more stitches and rows than called for in the instructions, knit another swatch with larger needles; if you have fewer stitches and rows, knit another swatch with smaller needles.

I-Cord (also called Knit-Cord)

This is worked with two double-pointed needles. Cast on the desired number of stitches (usually three to four). Knit across these stitches, then *without turning the needle, slide stitches to other end of needle, pull the yarn around the back, and knit the stitches as usual. Repeat from * for desired length.

Increases

Bar Increase

Knitwise (k1f&b)

Knit into a stitch but leave the stitch on the left needle (**Figure 1**), then knit through the back loop of the same stitch (**Figure 2**) and slip the original stitch off the needle (**Figure 3**).

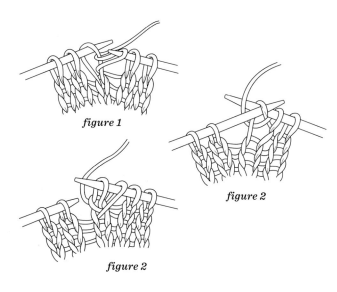

figure 1

figure 2

figure 2

Purlwise (p1f&b)

Work as for a knitwise bar increase, but purl into the front and back of the same stitch.

Raised Make-One (M1) Increase

Note: Use the left slant if no direction of slant is specified.

Left Slant (M1L)

With left needle tip, lift the strand between the last knitted stitch and the first stitch on the left needle from front to back (**Figure 1**), then knit the lifted loop through the back (**Figure 2**).

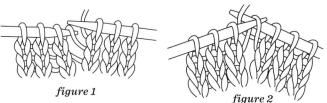

figure 1

figure 2

Right Slant (M1R)

With left needle tip, lift the strand between the needles from back to front (**Figure 1**). Knit the lifted loop through the front (**Figure 2**).

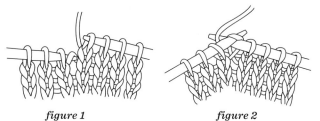

figure 1

figure 2

Purlwise (M1P)

With left needle tip, lift the strand between the needles from front to back (**Figure 1**), then purl the lifted loop through the back (**Figure 2**).

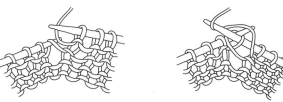

figure 1

figure 2

Magic-Loop Technique

Using a 32" or 40" (80 or 100 cm) circular needle, cast on the desired number of stitches. Slide the stitches to the center of the cable, then fold the cable and half of the stitches at the midpoint, then pull a loop of the cable between the stitches. Half of the stitches will be on one needle tip and the other half will be on the other tip (**Figure 1**). Hold the needle tips parallel so that the working yarn comes out of the right-hand edge of the back needle. *Pull the back needle tip out to expose about 6" (15 cm) of cable and use that needle to knit the stitches on the front needle (**Figure 2**). At the end of those stitches, pull the cable so that the two sets of stitches are at the ends of their respective needle tips, turn the work around and repeat from * to complete one round of knitting.

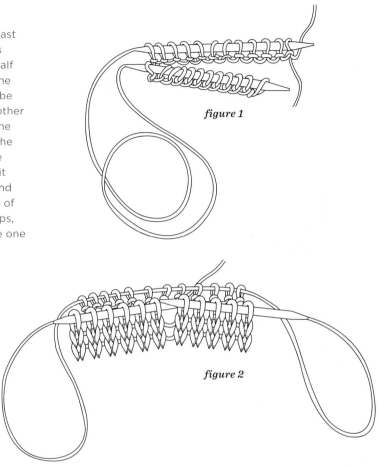

figure 1

figure 2

One-Row Buttonhole

With RS facing, bring yarn to front, slip the next stitch purlwise, return yarn to the back, *slip the next stitch purlwise, pass the first slipped stitch over the second slipped stitch and off the needle; repeat from * two more times (**Figure 1**). Slip the last stitch on the right needle tip to the left needle tip and turn the work so that the wrong side is facing. **With yarn in back, insert right needle tip between the first two stitches on the left needle tip (**Figure 2**), draw through a loop and place it on the left needle]; rep from ** three more times then turn the work so the right side is facing. With yarn in back, slip the first stitch and lift the extra cast-on stitch over the slipped stitch (**Figure 3**) and off the needle to complete the buttonhole.

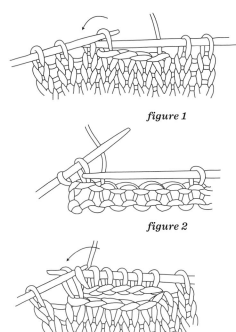

figure 1

figure 2

figure 3

Pick Up and Knit

Along CO or BO Edge

With right side facing and working from right to left, insert the tip of the needle into the center of the stitch below the bind-off or cast-on edge (**Figure 1**), wrap yarn around needle, and pull through a loop (**Figure 2**). Pick up one stitch for every existing stitch.

Along Shaped Edge

With right side facing and working from right to left, insert tip of needle between last and second-to-last stitches, wrap yarn around needle, and pull through a loop. Pick up and knit about three stitches for every four rows, adjusting as necessary so that picked-up edge lays flat.

figure 1

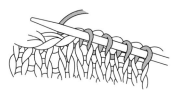

figure 2

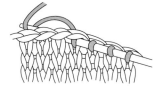

Short-Rows

Knit Side

Work to turning point, slip next stitch purlwise (**Figure 1**), bring the yarn to the front, then slip the same stitch back to the left needle (**Figure 2**), turn the work around and bring the yarn in position for the next stitch—one stitch has been wrapped, and the yarn is correctly positioned to work the next stitch. When you come to a wrapped stitch on a subsequent row, hide the wrap by working it together with the wrapped stitch as follows: Insert right needle tip under the wrap (from the front if wrapped stitch is a knit stitch; from the back if wrapped stitch is a purl stitch; **Figure 3**), then into the stitch on the needle, and work the stitch and its wrap together as a single stitch.

Purl Side

Work to the turning point, slip the next stitch purlwise to the right needle, bring the yarn to the back of the work (**Figure 1**), return the slipped stitch to the left needle, bring the yarn to the front between the needles (**Figure 2**), and turn the work so that the knit side is facing—one stitch has been wrapped, and the yarn is correctly positioned to knit the next stitch. To hide the wrap on a subsequent purl row, work to the wrapped stitch, use the tip of the right needle to pick up the wrap from the back, place it on the left needle (**Figure 3**), then purl it together with the wrapped stitch.

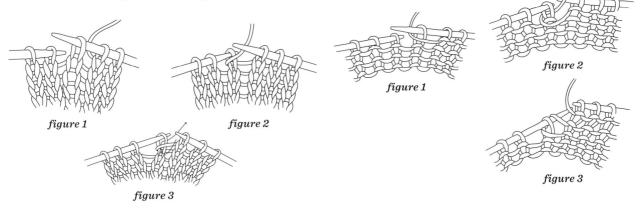

figure 1

figure 2

figure 3

figure 1

figure 2

figure 3

Weave in Loose Ends

Thread the ends on a tapestry needle and trace the path of a row of stitches (**Figure 1**) or work on the diagonal, catching the back side of the stitches (**Figure 2**). To reduce bulk, do not weave two ends in the same area. To keep color changes sharp, work the ends into areas of the same color.

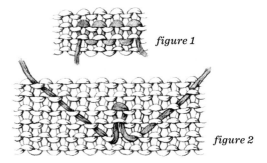

figure 1

figure 2

Sources for Yarn

BIJOU BASIN RANCH
PO Box 154
Elbert, CO 80106
bijoubasinranch.com

**BLUE SKY ALPACAS INC./
SPUD & CHLOË**
PO Box 88
Cedar, MN 55011
blueskyalpacas.com
spudandchloe.com

CASCADE YARNS
PO Box 58168
1224 Andover Park E.
Tukwila, WA 98188
cascadeyarns.com

CLASSIC ELITE YARNS
16 Esquire Rd., Unit 2
North Billerica, MA 01862-2500
classiceliteyarns.com

THE FIBRE COMPANY
2000 Manor Rd.
Conshohocken, PA 19428
thefibreco.com

GREEN MOUNTAIN SPINNERY
PO Box 568
7 Brickyard Ln.
Putney, VT 05346
spinnery.com

KNITPICKS
13118 NE 4th St.
Vancouver, WA 98684
knitpicks.com

**KNITTING FEVER INC./DEBBIE BLISS/
ELSEBETH LAVOLD**
PO Box 336
315 Bayview Ave.
Amityville, NY 11701
knittingfever.com
debbieblissonline.com

LOUET NORTH AMERICA
3425 Hands Rd.
Prescott, ON
Canada K0E 1T0
louet.com

QUINCE & COMPANY
85 York St.
Portland, ME 04101
quinceandco.com

TAHKI-STACY CHARLES INC.
70–30 80th St. Bldg. 12
Ridgewood, NY 11385
tahkistacycharles.com

TUNNEY WOOL COMPANY/O-WOOL
915 N. 28th St.
Philadelphia, PA 19130
o-wool.com

**WESTMINSTER FIBERS/ROWAN/
AMY BUTLER**
8 Shelter Dr.
Greer, SC 29650
westminsterfibers.com

Index

YOU DON'T HAVE TO BE FINISHED!

Here are a few must-have resources that will keep your knitting needles clicking all year long.

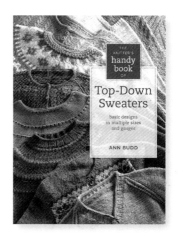

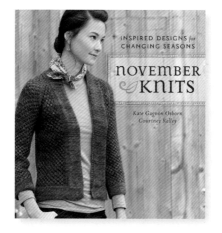

THE KNITTER'S
HANDY BOOK OF
TOP-DOWN SWEATERS
Basic Designs in Multiple
Sizes and Gauges

Ann Budd

ISBN 978-1-59668-483-6
$29.95

NOVEMBER KNITS
Inspired Designs for
Changing Seasons

*Courtney Kelley and
Kate Gagnon Osborn*

ISBN 978-1-59668-439-3
$24.95

WEEKEND HATS
25 Knitted Caps, Berets,
Cloches, and More

*Cecily Glowik MacDonald
and Melissa LaBarre*

ISBN 978-1-59668-438-6
$22.95